CW00505513

PRAISE

'With raw vulnerability, Olla beautifully captures the universal yearning for identity and a deep sense of belonging. With adventure and introspection, 'From Riyadh to Rio' offers invaluable insights and guidance to cultivate an authentic sense of belonging deep within our hearts.'

Dr. Shefali,
Clinical Psychologist and NYT Bestselling Author

'I don't know whether I love Olla more or the book more—it's going to be a toss-up. I read the entire book. I experienced all sorts of emotions—from tears of sorrow to tears of joy and everything in between. Olla is a brilliant storyteller on the stage and in the book. This book will not only make you think, but it will also touch your heart and soul.'

Rajesh Setty,
Author of 16 Published Books, Entrepreneur, and Bionic Comic

'From Riyadh to Rio' is a captivating exploration of navigating diverse cultures and beliefs, illuminating the complexities of self-identity in the process. With an important message for our era of global migration, this moving read urges us to embrace a profound sense of home no matter where our journeys take us.'

Marisa Peer,
Bestselling Author of 'Tell Yourself a Better Lie' and a Leading Therapist

'From Riyadh to Rio' is a gripping, mesmerizing coming-of-age tale of a young girl's transformational journey. It is an inspirational account whose raw honesty will grip you. It is a page-turner and heartwarming read.'

Dr. Srikumar Rao,
TED Speaker, Elite Coach, and Author of 4 grounding breaking books, including his most recent; "Modern Wisdom, Ancient Roots: The Movers and Shakers' Guide to Unstoppable Success"

'From Riyadh to Rio' is a beautifully written memoir about the reader as much as it is about the author. Olla takes us on her adventures to find her passion, find her voice, and find her 'home', and in the process, helps us to see how we can be courageous enough to do the same.'

Jason Goldberg,
Bestselling Author of "Prison Break," Celebrity Mental Performance Coach

'Olla is an incredible human being with an inspiring story that is a testament to her commitment to tap into her inner power and find the courage to share it with the world.'

Jimmy Naraine,
Author, Award-Winning Educator, Entrepreneur

'From Riyadh to Rio' is by far the most influential book I've ever read on the topic of finding 'home.' It's a must-read for anyone who has ever felt like they don't belong, or simply those who have a deep inner desire for wanderlust!'

Amy White,
Founder of The White Editorial and Editor

'Olla's beautiful book is filled with love and is truly "from the heart." You dive into it headlong and feel embraced in a caring hug. Enveloped in her beautiful poetic style, her deep wisdom hits you with force and conviction. It is a beautiful, warm, and profound journey as beautiful as the writer herself.'

Kristina Mand-Lakhiani,
Bestselling Author of 'Becoming Flawesome' and Co-founder of Mindvalley

FROM RIYADH TO RIO

OLLA ABBAS

FROM RIYADH
TO RIO

A Healing Journey Back Home
Through Cultures, Relationships,
Religions, and Love.

OLLA ABBAS

From Riyadh To Rio
Copyright © 2023 Olla Abbas
First published in 2023

Print: 978-1-76124-108-6
Print-colour: 978-1-76124-152-9
E-book: 978-1-76124-151-2
Hardback: 978-1-76124-150-5

All rights reserved. No part of this book may be reproduced, stored in a retrieval system, or transmitted by any means (electronic, mechanical, photocopying, recording, or otherwise) without written permission from the author.

Because of the dynamic nature of the Internet, any web addresses or links contained in this book may have changed since publication and may no longer be valid. The information in this book is based on the author's experiences and opinions. The views expressed in this book are solely those of the author and do not necessarily reflect the views of the publisher; the publisher hereby disclaims any responsibility for them.

The author of this book does not dispense any form of medical, legal, financial, or technical advise either directly or indirectly. The intent of the author is solely to provide information of a general nature to help you in your quest for personal development and growth. In the event you use any of the information in this book, the author and the publisher assume no responsibility for your actions. If any form of expert assistance is required, the services of a competent professional should be sought.

Publishing information
Publishing and design facilitated by Passionpreneur Publishing
A division of Passionpreneur Organization Pty Ltd
ABN: 48640637529

Melbourne, VIC | Australia
www.PassionpreneurPublishing.com

About
the Author

ABOUT THE AUTHOR

Born into a world of cultural confusion, Olla embarked on an extraordinary journey of self-discovery and profound transformation. As a second-generation immigrant, born and raised in a country she wasn't allowed to call her own, she grappled with the depths of her identity- embarking on an unyielding quest to find her rightful place in the tapestry of existence. Defying conventions, Olla fearlessly traversed 30+ countries, abandoning a promising career in Biomedical Engineering to pioneer transformative experiences that transcend borders, uniting people and fostering a profound sense of belonging.

Olla has a decade of experience in personal development, working with the world's biggest educational platform for personal and professional growth. Her dedication to growth and her relentless pursuit of deeper connections is evident in her everyday life.

Olla's authentic presence on stage captivated audiences when she spoke about; "What's like to be a Black, African, Muslim woman," "Your stories are the Lego bricks of your life," and "What is home?"—sharing the stage with world-renowned mentors such as

Vishen Lakhiani, Lisa Nichols, Michael Beckwith, and many more international Bestselling authors.

Fueling her unyielding passion to inspire others, Olla has crafted a testament to self-discovery and self-love. 'From Riyadh to Rio' is a breathtaking chronicle of adventure inviting readers to embrace their unique stories and cultivate a home within their mind, body, heart, and soul. Her vision for this volume is to reach anyone who is or has gone through a similar journey to use their story to unleash their highest potential and redefine their sense of home.

FROM THE HEART

Before we embark on this journey together, I express my heartfelt gratitude for the privilege of your time and the opportunity to share my story with you. Your presence here validates the countless hours I have dedicated to pouring my heart into these pages. Each word I hesitated to write and every story I feared to reveal, find solace in your willingness to give them a chance. From the depths of my being, thank you for being here.

It is important to note that every narrative, reflection, and conclusion in this account stems from my deeply personal experiences. Their purpose is not to form opinions, make sweeping statements or recommendations, or pass judgment on any place, city, or individual. Rather, they serve as a reflection of the encounters I have had and my own perception of the moments that have shaped my life.

Every city and every person mentioned along this journey has played a significant role in shaping the person I have become, for that, I am eternally grateful.

If any part of my story resonates with you, I hope you find solace in knowing that you are not alone and that every experience carries profound lessons. And if you have yet to encounter something similar, may you discover inspiration, reflection, or even a fleeting moment of joy within these pages.

In gratitude,
Olla

Let's stay connected!

To Mama and Papa,
you will always be the home that makes my soul smile.

To my siblings, Assgad, Abbas, Attaf, and Alyaa,
I am blessed to have you as my ride and
die on this journey.

Ronan, you are a gift.
Eternally grateful to come home to you.

To my extended Sudanese family navigating
the hardships of war with resilience, your boundless hearts
and kindness have been beacons of solace amidst
the darkest hours. May the world, in turn, mirror
your unwavering love and compassion.

CONTENT

FROM HOME

It was 2003. I sat among the towering piles of boxes that populated my once-cosy living room, and only then did it sink in: this was goodbye to the only home I'd ever known. Riyadh might not have been the land of my parent's birth, but it was mine. It would still be home until the moving van arrived.

The boxes, stacked high and teetering, held all my possessions, memories, and identity. My seventeen years of existence were now reduced to a messy pile of cardboard.

As I walked through the empty five-bedroom apartment, I was struck by its size and the echoes of laughter that once filled its rooms. I stood in my old bedroom, imagining how it once was—the tiny balcony where I sipped my morning coffee, my cluttered closet, my boombox blasting Backstreet Boys, and the white retro telephone that connected me to my friends. I giggled at the memory of us dancing and singing, trying to keep up with the beat.

'There is so much that I will miss from Riyadh,' I remember thinking to myself. Leaving Riyadh meant leaving behind joy-filled Thursday park days with my family, shopping sprees, and the most delicious Shawarma I'd ever tasted. But most of all, I felt like I was leaving behind a part of myself. The thought of returning to my 'real' home—a place that only existed as a word on my passport—and departing the city that held all my memories was overwhelming. But that was the reality I had to face. It was time to go.

As I said goodbye, I had no idea that this single utterance of the word would mark the beginning of an adventure that would take me through uncharted territories far beyond the familiar walls of my childhood home, and it would redefine who I was and who I was meant to be. This was the birth of a transformative journey that would change my life forever.

From

Riyadh

CHAPTER 1

FROM RIYADH

'This is home, but not really home'

Growing up in the city of Riyadh in the 1980s felt as normal as could be, just like growing up anywhere else in the world. Riyadh was my home, and life at home was good. Everything was abundant, and almost everyone I knew seemed to have a pretty good life.

My father, Mohammed, had moved to Riyadh a couple of years after he graduated from university in Khartoum. At the age of twenty-eight, he received a generous job offer as a Pharmaceutical Manager that meant he would start a completely new life. With his perfectly groomed (and colossal) afro, dark brown skin, and sharp sense of style, my dad's swag was undeniable. He was of average height, but his afro made him seem taller than the numbers would state. He had a snub nose, a luminous smile, and black diamond eyes that radiated 'you are welcome here,' to anyone who locked eyes with him.

Everyone who knew my dad then would agree that he was one of those people you fall in love with, within the first five minutes. And he still is. Light of spirits, with a smile across his face all the time.

Dad didn't worry about small things. I don't remember ever seeing him stressed or anxious; he'd be cracking jokes even when things were difficult, and he gave the impression of always having everything under control, in a way that I found very comforting. To me, he is like 'a warm blanket on a chilly day,' because that's how he makes me feel every time he is around. As a girl, I always felt warm and taken care of. I felt safe to express my thoughts whenever I was with him. If The Jackson 5 and Nelson Mandela miraculously had a baby, that would be my dad.

Dad was also a good provider for his family of five children and my mum, Eman. We had a beautiful home, housekeepers, regular shopping sprees, always the best education, and summer travel; it would be fair to say we lived in abundance. Some would have even described our lifestyle as 'rich,' but to be rich in Saudi was to have luxury cars parked in the driveway of your palace; I always considered us as 'second class.'

My mother made sure to remind us we weren't rich. She managed the family finances with the precision of an accountant, always ensuring we weren't being too spoiled. Whenever I needed to ask for extra money, I had to deliver a detailed explanation of what the money was for, and why this 'new thing' was of importance to my life. Whenever my siblings and I couldn't articulate a valid reason to ask for money, we didn't get it. That taught me two things: first, that money is a serious business, and second, that I had to use persuasion to get what I wanted. I had no idea back then how well this skill would serve me later in life.

Born in the sixties in Port Sudan, Mum was tall and caramel-skinned, with curves that waved effortlessly like the ocean. Her flawless skin, prominent brown eyes, and toothpaste-ad smile made her features hard not to stare at. She would always stand in perfect posture. Ever stern and often strict, but never unkind. When my mum started university, she needed a job to support herself. She was very passionate about the idea of becoming a TV host, and while she had no formal training or experience in the field whatsoever, she had huge amounts of determination. As soon as she arrived in the capital city of Khartoum, she applied for a part-time position as a TV host and got the job in her first interview. By the early '80s, Mum had become a well-known TV host in Sudan.

I still look at the magazine with my mother on the cover—we've kept it as sacred pieces of family history. Every time I revisit it, I feel the same pride I felt when I was a child. My mother was also what I would describe as a knowledge enthusiast. During her twenties, she moved from her home city, Port Sudan, to Khartoum to further her education in Philosophy, then Strategic Sciences, and finally, Technology Education.

She has always been known for her entrepreneurial spirit and strong personality, the kind of person who would not waste time sugar-coating what needed to be said—which makes her seem scary to many.

They are probably right to fear her, for my mother is fierce.

When Mum was in her twenties, she lost her sister to tragic medical negligence. She and her sister were a few years apart in age, and they had been best friends since childhood. The hospital where the incident occurred rapidly covered up the situation to protect its name. But my mum wouldn't have been my mum if she had simply let it go. She wrote several articles about what happened and managed to get them published in national newspapers. All this was long before she had a name on TV or a brand as a TV anchor.

Not long after, the hospital dared to sue her for the articles published, but she refused to settle or retract, instead deciding to take the case to court. After months of nasty legal arguments, the case was resolved in favour of Eman Helal, my fearless mother.

Love Happens

Mum and Dad met at a dinner party hosted by a common friend. During the first hour of the gathering, while people were mingling and getting to know each other, my mother kept hearing a man's loud laughter. It made its way to her all the way along the hallway and disrupted her conversation. She tried seeing who the man was, so she could avoid him later, but from a distance, she was only able to catch his Afro, his tight white shirt, and his matching white bell-bottom pants.

Soon everyone was asked to grab a seat at a long rectangular dinner table, and to my mother's great surprise, the man she wanted to avoid sat exactly opposite her. 'Oh, come on,' she thought to herself;

but the giant smile across his face and his kind eyes made her decide to give him another chance.

Thirty minutes into dinner, everyone was very deep into their conversations with their new acquaintances; my mum chit-chatted jovially with the people to her left and her right. At some point, she made a brief pause to take a sip of water, and her eyes met his for the first time. He took his chance and asked her a question that became a conversation. The next thing they knew, they had been chatting for hours. The people at that gathering became friends and continued to hang out regularly as a group, including Mum and Dad, who remained good friends—only friends—for about two years.

But the more time they spent together, the more their connection and emotions deepened. In their third year of friendship, they finally confessed their feelings and started dating. Every time my mother saw the yellow Volkswagen Beetle making its way to pick her up, butterflies danced in her stomach. And when my dad got out to open the car door for her, grinning from ear to ear, the butterflies were joined by her heart skipping beats.

He always looked as sharp as a blade, ready to slice hearts across the city. Every time she came back from meeting him, her heart felt a little fuller with love. At the end of that year, my father popped the question, and they got married. Forty years later, Mum said, and I quote, 'If I were taken back in time and asked to choose my life partner, I would choose him over and over again.'

Having grown up knowing my parents' life story, I am deeply influenced by their characters, which have profoundly shaped my personality. I have always aspired to emulate my dad's kindness and calmness and my mother's confidence and fierceness. Over the years, observing their relationship has instilled in me a genuine belief in the power of enduring love that is strong, unwavering, and kind.

Witnessing the unconditional love and care my parents bestowed upon each other, and the family they created, has left a lasting impression on me. While they were not without flaws, like any other parents, they set a high standard for a committed relationship and emphasized the significance of family and home.

Our Family

I grew up as the middle child, with two brothers and two sisters. I had a good relationship with my siblings. We always had a subconscious silent agreement: to survive peacefully at home, we would respect each other's privacy, cover up for one another, and join forces to accomplish goals our parents wouldn't agree to. Let me tell you, that strategy worked like magic.

The environment in our house was full-on Sudanese. My parents made sure we constantly experienced Sudanese culture through all our five senses. We grew up listening to them speaking only the Arabic-Sudanese dialect; Sudanese art pieces decorated our home; Sudanese Bakhoor (traditional wood chips that smell like a piece of heaven) dominated the house with scent; and we often enjoyed authentic Sudanese cuisine that consisted of generous amounts of stews and gravies.

At least eighty percent of the family friends who visited our home were of Sudanese origin, and we regularly attended Sudanese celebrations in Riyadh. These celebrations followed Sudanese traditions, of course, and there was no gender separation. My parents continued to follow Sudanese customs as much as they could. In a sense, my parents created a 'Little Sudan' in Riyadh.

For us kids, the story had another side. From an early age, we came to understand that we were not fully 'Saudi.' Everyone around us referred to us as Sudanese, even though we didn't live in Sudan. Our family and friends who were born and raised there never referred to themselves as Saudi or even 'half-Saudi.' There was this obvious unspoken rule for all of us born in Riyadh to immigrant parents: This is home … but not **really** home.

No matter how hard our parents tried to instil Sudanese culture, once we stepped outside our home, we met different people, spoke different dialects, and engaged in different customs. As a kid, I didn't want to stand out or be different. I wanted to blend in, so I would naturally adapt the way I spoke, what topics I spoke about, the way I dressed, and how I behaved based on the surroundings I found myself in. I would unconsciously switch between identities to adapt to the environment around me.

Unlike our parents, being fully Sudanese and only Sudanese wasn't possible for my siblings and me. Many aspects of Sudanese culture simply didn't make sense in Riyadh—and they didn't make sense to us. We were absorbing so much more from the world around us.

As my siblings and I got older and started to develop our personalities, our culture at home became more neutral. My parents stopped asking us to join them on visits to their Sudanese friends (and their friends' kids); they stopped asking us to dress a certain way, attend all cultural events, or call the entire extended family in Sudan every time a wedding or funeral took place. Everyone did what they were comfortable with, and that kept the peace at home.

My father and I always had a very special relationship. He was easy to approach because he was never judgmental. He never became overly emotional or overreacted to situations. Usually, he supported my choices, regardless of how nonsensical they may have been, so much so that my mum used to call me what translated to 'his second wife.' She used to say, 'He obeys more of your wishes than mine.' I didn't agree with her statement, nor did I like it—although I did agree that our relationship was exceptional.

My mother was the mature one among the three of us. She rejected most of our ideas and deemed them unnecessary. As a result, we secretly baked our plans and presented them to her only when they were ready.

Growing up, I was always a curious kid who wanted to try new things. I was not afraid of looking like an idiot when putting myself in situations where I was completely clueless. My passion blinded me, so that I would pursue that one thing I wanted. Nothing was able to stand in my way. Even though I got my curiosity and this sense of persistence from my mum, that didn't keep me from being the 'little rebel' in my family.

I had a hard time settling for things just because the adults in my life told me to. That was the case with my education, for example. While most of the kids we knew stayed in one school, I changed schools many times. For some reason, I just couldn't settle into the system. The rules, the activities, the teachers—something made me feel there should be something more to it … so I kept searching.

My dad always wanted to provide the best education for me and my siblings. Even though public schools in Riyadh seemed to be just fine, Dad enrolled us in private schools. The only problem was that these schools were expensive compared to public schools, so only a small number of kids went to them. My secondary school was called 'Al Morabaa'—a cute school that was located in our neighbourhood. Girls' schools in Riyadh had high walls, so people on the outside wouldn't be able to see the girls. A single white building held all the classrooms. And there was a small garden in front of the entrance.

I will never forget my shock on the first day of secondary school. I walked into a big classroom where there was a blackboard, a grey desk for the teacher, and four desks arranged in a row in the middle of this huge room. The arrangement of the class got me a bit confused, so I stepped back to take another look at the sign on the door to make sure I was in the right place. The sign said: *Awal Metwasit*, which translates to 'Secondary first.' It was indeed the correct class: my class had a total of four students, including me. FOUR!

You would think that a smaller class is much better because it's more intimate; the kids can get close to one another, and the teachers can offer more individual focus on each student. Sadly, that was not the case.

During my time there, I didn't make a single friend. The kids all kept to themselves during classes, and when it was time for the break, they disappeared into the flood of girls in the canteen and the lunch area.

Every morning, I resented going to school. When I was there, I felt like my organs were slowly dying one at a time from boredom. I also really hated the fact that I had to cover myself from head to toe with a black cloth called an *abaya* to enter the school. The schools in Riyadh were single-sex institutions, so we didn't need to cover ourselves while we were inside the school, just when we left and when we entered. There was a guard at the gate making sure you were completely covered from head to toe. And heaven forbid if you had any bit of skin showing … you would not be allowed in. It was only a few minutes each day, but those few minutes felt like an eternity.

I knew my dad also hated the fact that I had to cover my face, so I played on that. Every time he came to pick me up and asked 'how was your day today?' I would exaggerate how awful it had been, hoping that one day it would get to him, and he would take me out of that school. And sure enough, that day eventually came.

I remember it well: I was in class finishing an exercise when the teacher came and asked me to pack my things and head to the principal's office. As I walked there, I was nervously trying to think of what I might have done wrong. As soon as I stepped inside the room, it was easy to see that the principal wasn't in her best mood. She said, 'I had a chat with your father, and we both agreed that you shouldn't continue in this school. Please make sure you take all your belongings. Your father is waiting for you outside.'

I rushed towards the main gate (not covering my face). Before the guard could say anything, I ran toward Dad. 'What happened?' I asked enthusiastically.

Dad calmly switched on the car engine and said, 'I argued with the principal, and she was very unprofessional. I don't see this place as being fit to teach you anything.' I couldn't stop smiling. 'So which school do you want to go to?' Dad asked, and the question felt like music to my ears. I thought to myself, 'I get to choose the school!? Mission accomplished!'

At this time, my mum was in Khartoum taking care of her business. We knew she would flip out because schools might not allow me to join in the middle of the year. So Dad and I decided it was best to fix the situation first and only then present the cake we baked. 'I want to join an English school,' I said.

My dad responded immediately without further questioning. 'Be ready by 9 am tomorrow.'

We went to 'Manarat Al Riyadh' first, one of the most prestigious English schools in the city. It was evident that the principal was shocked at my request to join Grade 8 when I barely spoke any English. She explained that it was impossible to put me in the same grade I had left with my poor English proficiency. She advised that I start from Grade 6, so I could catch up to the rest of the kids. Ignoring two academic years from my life wasn't an option for my father. So, we drove to the next English school on our list, and then the next. At each, we got the same answer.

On our way back home, Dad remembered there was one more English school close to our house called the Diplomatic International School. With little hope remaining, we walked to the principal's office. A Pakistani man in his forties in a grey suit sat at a big wooden desk looking at documents. He lifted his head as we walked in, and his face immediately assumed a giant smile. He rushed out of his chair and gave my father a very warm welcome. It was clear that they were acquainted.

As it turned out, Principal Zain had worked with Dad a couple of years earlier, and they had a good relationship. After they caught up for about thirty minutes, Dad shared my story and told him how passionate I was to learn English. Principal Zain stood up from his chair, walked outside, and came back with twelve books that he displayed on the table in front of me. 'School starts at 7.30 am tomorrow,' he said. 'Please don't be late.'

On the first day at my new school, I didn't speak to anyone because I simply had no means of communication. The teacher strategically positioned me in class next to a Lebanese girl who spoke fluent Arabic and English. The first class was Physics. The whole time, I was trying hard to catch any words the teacher was saying that I might recognise. When that failed, I tried to decipher her body language, hoping it could help me figure out what the lesson was about. But that didn't work either.

I guess 'confused' was showing all over my face; the teacher called me out and said, 'Olla, are you following?' The only problem with her question was that I didn't know what 'following' meant, so I kept quiet. Tension in the room started to rise in the silence. Slowly,

I witnessed faces turning in my direction—one face at a time. Not able to take the awkwardness of the moment any longer, the Lebanese girl leaned closer and translated the question. I looked at the teacher and said, 'Yes!' Her eyes filled with scepticism, she turned back to the blackboard and continued the class.

For the next couple of months, my father and I would sit after school for hours to go through each lesson I'd had that day. He would first translate each word, explain the lesson in Arabic, ask me to memorize the new terminologies in English, and finally explain the whole lesson in English. We did this every single day.

I started reading novels, watching shows and movies, anything I could do to get better at English. With time, the improvement was evident. Every time I heard a Backstreet Boys song and understood some of the lyrics, it felt like a moment of victory. The more I understood, the more I felt the power of my independence. Learning English opened a whole new world for me.

Language wasn't the only challenge I faced when I joined the international school. Having been in a girls' school until then, I was extremely shy to do any kind of human activities with so many boys around. Eating, talking, and laughing were impossible without being self-conscious. But the worst activity of all was playing sports.

Until the eighth grade, I had never engaged in any physical activity whatsoever—to the point that I didn't even *know* that I hadn't engaged in any physical activity. At the Saudi school, the extracurricular activities for girls were cooking, painting, and knitting. I didn't know a single girl in my circle of friends or community who went to a gym or did sports, as a hobby. So when I joined the mixed school, I hadn't even jogged a day in my life. And the last thing I wanted was to do it in front of the opposite gender.

After years of being told sports were for boys, I believed that girls who ran around looked less ladylike and a little idiotic. So, while the other, 'normal,' kids couldn't wait for P.E. class, I dreaded it. In my first one, I prayed that the teacher wouldn't ask me to play basketball with the team. I felt that I'd make a fool out of myself. With time, that stress lessened, but I still didn't join any basketball games. I was so far behind everyone that no one wanted me to play with them anyway. It was a kind of win-win situation.

After another day at my new school, my mum came back from Sudan excited to share all the stories about her business trip. She was still completely clueless that I had not only changed schools but curriculums. As much as we didn't want to burst her happy bubble, we knew we would have to, eventually. And when she was finally done reporting all her adventures, Dad broke the news to her.

As expected, she was furious. She couldn't believe the damage we were capable of doing when left unattended for two short months. Her biggest worry was that I wouldn't be able to pick up my grades, and that I would graduate with low scores, reducing my opportunities to go to university. But the damage was done, and it was too late to reverse it. After a couple of weeks, my mother surrendered to reality.

Two years later, I was standing on the stage in the school courtyard, waiting to receive an award for scoring second-best in my class. My dad was sitting in the audience, grinning from ear to ear. As the principal called my name and I walked over to receive my golden trophy and pose for a picture, all I could see was my dad. We both smiled and in our hearts, I know we were both saying, 'We did it.'

After graduating from the tenth grade, my friends and I decided to leave school and focus on preparing for the Cambridge IGCSE (The International General Certificate of Secondary Education) examination, which was one of the toughest in the world. Doing home tuition was life-changing. I had complete control of my daily schedule and started and ended the day as I pleased. On one of my lazy days, I woke up late in the afternoon, after having gone to bed at 3 am the night before. With my entire body still aching and trying to start operating, I dragged myself to the bathroom. As I finished brushing my teeth and reached for the face towel that hung in front of me, I felt the sudden presence of another person entering the bathroom.

I turned around to see which one of my annoying siblings it was. Instead, I saw the man who would occasionally come to our home to help with the cleaning. He was a huge South-Asian man, whose eyes flared with malice every time he looked at me. And there he was, in the small space of the bathroom hall, his body dangerously close to mine and his eyes flaring as they always did.

My heart dropped to my feet. I had a sudden urge to run away as something in my system recognised the unmistakable feeling of danger. Before I could move, he grabbed my thigh with one of his massive hands. I felt a surge of crippling electricity run through my body. With all the power I was able to generate, I managed to push him away and make enough space between us to escape.

I sprinted through our home in some sort of adrenaline shock, which only settled down once I reached my mum, who was cooking in the kitchen. My brain commanded me to speak, but only a swirl of muddled words came out of my mouth. I sounded like I was speaking another language, but even then, Mum knew exactly what I was trying to say.

She rushed to the bathroom, where the man was pretending to clean. I was sweating and hyperventilating as I followed my mother closely to make sure I wouldn't miss what was about to happen. For the first time in my life, I was grateful that people found my mother scary.

'What did you just do? My daughter said you touched her,' Mum said firmly.

The man stopped cleaning and blurted out some words to defend himself in his broken Arabic: 'No madame, me just trying to get the trash bin when I touched her leg. This accident.' I waited to see whether my mother would decide to throw something at him or punch him straight in the face before she kicked him out of the house, but she just stood there.

She finally turned to me and said: 'Go to your room and stay away from where he works.'

Everything around me stood still.

It took me a minute before I could fully grasp what she had just said. I repeated slowly, looking her right in the eye: 'Stay away from where he works? You're keeping him here?' I stared at her in disbelief, as her silence confirmed that the man would stay in the house and finish his work.

I ran to my room shouting, 'I will tell Dad!' and slammed my room door shut so that the entire building could hear. My fear quickly escalated into rage. I fell to the ground crying, feeling defeated, helpless, furious, and confused. I didn't understand. I was certain that my mother would have yelled at him and thrown him out of the house. I was certain my fearless mother would protect me.

The scene of him vigorously grasping my thigh played over and over in my head, and every time it did, I would feel electricity sweep through my spine. My stomach twisted. I wished I could amputate the leg he had grabbed.

Any negative thought that ever existed was invited into my mind that day. I wanted to scream, to break things, to punch him, to yell at my mum, to cry, to hurt myself—all at the same time. My head dropped to the floor as I cried. I stayed in the same fetal position on the floor for hours.

The question that kept coming to my mind was, 'Do I tell my dad?' My heart told me that I should because he would respond differently than Mum had. But my mind argued that I had been 'certain' about my mum's reaction too, so maybe I should save myself another disappointment. And when I imagined telling my dad, I cringed at the thought of confessing a man had touched me. A part of me felt ashamed even to say those words. In a culture where such topics are taboo, it is harder to describe an incident like that.

My parents had never said a single word about anything sexual in our household. With no one mentioning it, I intuitively grew up believing that anything to do with sex was forbidden. Even talking about it felt sinful and vulgar. As a woman, my sexuality felt like a weapon of mass destruction that I had to try my best to cover and hide. The only place where I knew sex was allowed, and where it was elevated into something close to holy, was within the sacred bonds of marriage.

In hindsight, I can see that our cultural beliefs were trying to define sex as sacred, but all the wrong tools were being used to deliver that message. Fear and shame dominated; they kept us away from sex, making it almost impossible to ask questions or express any kind of thoughts related to the topic. Even when our safety was involved, we didn't know if we could ask for help or if we should be shamed for it. Reflecting back, I realised it was the very reason that prevented my mother from taking action towards the situation.

After much pondering, I finally decided against telling my father. Since I couldn't reach out to the people around me for help, I recruited myself for the job. Moving forward, I would handle any such situations on my own. And this became one of many secrets I kept.

Secrets

Secrets were the one thing I learned even before I knew the actual meaning of the word. I was just a little girl when I learned to keep my first secret, and as I grew, my secrets grew with me. I don't remember most of my early childhood, but I remember that. There are fragments of episodes here and there in my head, and for some reason, the ones that I recall are advising me not to dig deeper.

I remember, for example, at about five or six years of age, hiding in my father's closet among the hanging suits early in the morning. If not there, I would be hiding under a white dining table. It wasn't because I was playing hide and seek with my siblings—it was to keep myself safe. Although I was very young and didn't understand what was happening, I knew it wasn't right.

About weekly in the morning, right before my father left for work, I would hear him walk into the kitchen for his morning tea, and then the doorbell would ring. My eyes would widen at the sound. A family relative would then be greeted by my dad and invited into the house. He was a tall, yellowish-skinned man, with dark facial hair that covered half of his face. He must have been in his thirties back then. His technique was to arrive right before Dad left, so he had someone to open the door for him. At the same time, it was early enough for him to have the house all to himself, as my mother usually slept in the mornings.

I remember he would enjoy wandering around the house doing whatever he pleased before my mum woke up. My parents trusted him, as a close family member, so they would leave him unattended. It's crazy how sometimes the people close to us can be the same people we should be keeping an eye on.

The minute I heard his voice greeting my father, I would run and hide. This day, I chose the closet, hoping he wouldn't figure out where I was, and as I was holding on to that wish, I heard his footsteps approaching my parent's room. They came closer and closer. I closed my eyes as he opened the closet door and said, 'Are you hiding from your uncle?'

My memory reaches this part of the episode and goes no further. I have no images of what happened next, and honestly, I'm not trying hard to remember. Maybe something happened, and maybe it didn't. All I know is that whatever happened was not right … and so I kept it a secret.

In addition to secrets, I learned a new feeling, or rather, it was one I had never experienced to this magnitude before: hate. The male cleaner kept coming back to the house, and so did my uncle. I never knew I could hate other human beings as much as I hated the men who were permitted to invade my home every day.

Every time the cleaner passed me, he smirked as if to say: 'I am still here and there is nothing you can do about it.' His smirk made a ball of fire burn in my chest. I constantly prayed that the new housekeeper we'd hired would arrive sooner than we expected. And that day did finally arrive, and the male cleaner was gone forever. I was relieved to have my home back and put this incident behind me so I would never remember it again … or at least that's what I thought would happen.

Goodbyes

Upon completing the final exams of my school year, the path to college was the obvious next step, marking not just an academic transition but a bittersweet departure from Riyadh.

Although I had spent my entire life until that point in the embrace of this city, my status as the child of immigrant parents cast a shadow over my eligibility for citizenship and, consequently, for Saudi's public universities. The options were limited—only one private institution extended its doors to non-Saudi citizens, offering a sparse array of majors. Many like me were compelled to seek higher education beyond its borders.

The path to college carried a blend of sweet and bitter emotions. Excitement tinged as I envisioned discovering the treasures of a new country. Simultaneously, a twinge of sadness nipped at my heels. Departing Riyadh implied a detachment, for once I crossed its borders, I would lose my residency, and I would become obsolete in the system—as if I had never lived a day in Riyadh. My return would hinge on the threads of a tourist visa. The abrupt conversion from resident to visitor was hard to swallow.

During those pivotal moments, I observed acquaintances and friends dispersing like dandelion seeds, carried away by their pursuit of education on foreign grounds. As I contemplated my own path, my parents took a decision that would reverberate through our lives—a return to their homeland of Sudan.

Sudan's rising economy drew numerous Sudanese families back, like a magnetic pull, in the early 2000s. For my parents, Riyadh was a waypoint, not the final destination. They held a quiet understanding that their journey would eventually take them back to Sudan. Since our residency depended upon my father's work visa, we had no choice but to relocate to Sudan. With almost two decades of Riyadh imprinted in our memories, the time had come to say Goodbye.

And so, I found myself standing in the empty apartment, enveloped by stacks of cardboard boxes.

The continuous abundance the city had offered me all those years was undeniable, yet living as a foreigner at home for the rest of my life didn't resonate either. Being at the mercy of a colourful sticker called a visa that dictated my fate was no way to live. As uncomfortable as it was to change our lives completely, it was a chance for a new 'real' home. In Khartoum, I would belong, effortlessly, and I could live with my loved ones for as long as my heart desired.

Little did I know that my faith would change at the hands of a Sudanese guard with a lash.

From
Khartoum

CHAPTER 2

F<small>ROM</small> K<small>HARTOUM</small>

'Think inside the box'

Moving to Khartoum was a significant change for us. My parents had spent twenty-five years in Riyadh, the only home we kids had known. Despite being exposed to Sudanese culture throughout our lives and visiting Khartoum during school holidays, settling there permanently was a whole new experience for us.

The vast country of Sudan was diverse and had so much to offer. From north to south, the people of Sudan came in all colours, shapes, and dialects. My parents hailed from different cities—my mother from Port Sudan in the east, and my father from Wad Madani, the capital of the Al Jazirah state in east-central Sudan—and both had large families.

Khartoum is a beautiful city where the Blue Nile meets the White Nile, dividing it into three areas: Khartoum, Bahri, and Omdurman. Our house awaited us in Bahri. It was impossible to anticipate what my new life would be like. A part of me was excited to get to know the place that had been referred to as my 'home' all my life, another part was anxious about the unknown.

I remember when the car stopped in front of our white and maroon, two-story house in Bahri. I stood before the entrance gate while my dad unloaded the luggage, and I felt a knot in my stomach. This was not another trip where I got to be a tourist; this was our new house where we would wake up every morning.

As we went inside, each of us went in different directions, exploring. The house was fully furnished. Some furniture still had plastic covers. The house had everything, carpets, complete kitchenware, even towels. It was evident that for years my parents were hand-picking every item of this house in preparation for this moment.

As soon as word got out that we had arrived in Khartoum, the place became a kind of national parade. Families from both sides, friends, neighbours—everyone came to share their joy and welcome us. As in many houses in Khartoum, a rope was attached to our entrance door lock so people could open it from the outside without needing to ring the doorbell. Relatives and friends would walk into the living room or house salon uninvited, calling out '*Ya Nas Al Bait*' or '*Al Salam Alikum*' to tell us they had entered the house.

Whenever I heard a voice, I would run to my room and hide to prepare myself mentally to meet someone new. Making people feel welcome at any time is an act of kindness that I admire, but I was not used to it. Riyadh was more reserved. We never had anyone come unannounced, and neither did we have this many people come to visit regularly. So for the first months, I did a lot of running and hiding.

Outside the house was a new world I wanted to explore. In Khartoum, I tried public transportation for the first time. Taking a *raksha*, a motorized rickshaw (also widely known as a *tuk-tuk*), to the local *souq* with my cousin was an adventure in and of itself. I also did something I had been waiting for years to try, having tea by the Nile River served by *Sit Al Chai*, which translates to 'tea lady.' It was (and still is) a cultural experience. Her mini cafe, hand-made with old-school Pepsi bottle boxes, stole my heart.

Discovering the city of Khartoum was an unexpected delight; it was full of surprises, from the bustling markets overflowing with natural beauty products to the mouth-watering organic food. I became enamoured of the simple pleasures of life, like the daily milk delivery by a man on a donkey or the local street vendors selling superfoods like Balboa. Khartoum didn't have fancy buildings or cars, but a different and undeniable type of richness existed there.

Arab-Educated

Just a couple of months in, I quickly understood that life in Khartoum survived on only one thing: social bonds. The true heart of the city lay in its people. The Sudanese are renowned for their warmth, generosity, and kindness, which was evident in every aspect of daily life. It was simple: people cherished people there.

Everyone was responsible for building and maintaining strong social bonds with everyone around them, from neighbours and friends to all of one's nearby family members. It was compulsory to visit them regularly and attend every occasion—the happy ones and otherwise.

The community-driven life in Khartoum was beautiful, but it came with a hefty price tag. Within a few months, I felt like I was getting sucked into endless social responsibilities.

At first, I tried to keep up with all the family visits and events, but the more I participated, the more I felt suffocated by the expectations and commitments. I soon found myself skipping more and more of these events until I finally reached a point where I couldn't force myself to do things that went against my nature. The more I said no, the more I heard the phrase: 'But what will your uncle/aunt/cousin/uncle's neighbour think?'

While people cherished people in Khartoum, they also lived for people—another thing I learned early on. Reputation was a serious business. And I am not talking about difficult situations only, where someone has a reputation as a thief or a criminal, for example. Your reputation includes how well your children are doing in school, how old you were when you got married, and how many family occasions you skipped without a valid reason—it all counts.

I felt that if I were to make a small or a major life decision in Khartoum, I needed to consider everyone's approval before mine. You needed to think inside the box. And the box was a very tight space, dictating how creative you could get with your life, especially if you were a woman.

The more conversations I had in Khartoum, the more I understood one primary rule—your growth and success as a woman was tied to one goal: getting married and raising children. I could be the first Sudanese woman ever to land on the moon, but that wouldn't mean a thing if I didn't find a husband. My curious mind resisted many of these visions. The more I spent time with people, the more out of place I felt. And I didn't mind being classified as *Shehada Arabyia*. This term identified kids born and raised outside of Sudan. Its literal translation is 'Arab-educated.'

If you are categorized as *Shehada Arabyia*, you are regarded as a spoiled brat who would be clueless about street slang and unable to hustle a day in Sudan. So, a part of my 'reputation' was already figured out before I even arrived. And honestly, I didn't argue much with it. Maybe I *was* spoiled. I had never done my own laundry … let alone hustle. The truth is that I did feel different. I didn't vibe with most of the things that were the norm, with the cultural concepts about how I should live my life. The blueprint of how I should dress, think, behave, and speak could have been more appealing to me. I wanted to do and be more than what was asked of me. The curious little kid in me wanted more.

As someone raised in a multicultural environment, I was no stranger to adapting to my surroundings and changing my identity to fit in. Shifting identities as necessary had served me well, so *surviving* in Khartoum was not an issue. The real problem was that I wanted to *thrive*, and I knew it would be very challenging to do so there.

A Date with Destiny

One time, a few of my cousins and I decided to go for a movie night. Riyadh had no cinemas when I lived there, so going to the cinema for the first time was an exhilarating prospect. At the ticket counter, we were divided into two queues, one for women and the other for men. I volunteered to queue for us all, as the women's line was much shorter. When I got closer to the ticket counter, my cousin realised he had forgotten to pass me the money. He rushed to where I was standing and reached into his pocket to give me the cash.

A security guard shouted from a distance, 'Get away from the lady's line!'

'I just need a minute, please,' my cousin responded respectfully. The next thing I knew, the guard pushed my cousin to the floor by his shirt collar. The guard then took out a lash and swiped him with it.

It took me a second to interpret what was happening. My heart went from 0 to 100 in a second. I usually freeze in situations like this, but by the time the guard was going for the second round of lashing, I ran towards my cousin, screaming, 'STOP NOW!' and kneeled to the floor to pick up my cousin. When the guard saw me, he stopped and walked away.

My heart continued racing for hours after the incident. When it would slow down, an image of the guard throwing my cousin to the floor would make it run at full speed again. I was deeply shocked and saddened by the brutality of that man. To witness his hate towards a young person who could be his son's age and for no reason! I couldn't understand why anyone would treat another human that way.

My cousin, who was in his early twenties, was shocked at first, but he brushed it off—faster than he should have. What sucked was how we all knew there was nothing we could do about it. This sort of incident is not uncommon in Sudan. Human rights were under the feet of a regime that had been in place for decades; my parents and family members had always complained about that. The violation of human rights by the government kept Sudan at the lowest possible ranking in the world. Violence was how people in power kept others in constant fear of acting or speaking up.

And the crazy thing was that none of us said anything when we returned home, not to our parents, friends, or anyone. For some reason, we all just remained silent and carried on.

Since coming to Khartoum, I had been trying to make it feel like my 'home'—as everyone kept telling me. Deep inside, I had a lot of conflicting feelings. I had been open to giving the city a chance, but after that incident, I wasn't anymore. Coming face to face with the dark side of Sudan stirred my soul, and my heart made a decision as I lay in bed and stared at the ceiling that night. Khartoum would not be the place where my dreams would unfold. Yes, I had my 'roots,' but I had no soil to protect them.

'But if this is not home, where is it?' I felt my heart ache at the thought.

In that moment of pain, I knew I had a quest. I'd stop at nothing to find a place to call home.

Let the Journey Begin

Until then, I had only been somewhat excited to go to college. I felt drawn only to a few majors that universities offer. My passion had been to become a makeup artist, which my dad supported, but my mum thought it was more of a hobby than a successful career path. Then I realised that going to college was my ticket out of Khartoum.

I started researching different universities online and browsing through their various courses, like a McDonald's menu, hoping to find something interesting. The more I read about each course, the more I lost my brain cells to boredom. Nothing I read was intriguing to me. One day, while I was doing my research, my attention was distracted by a cheesy ad song playing on the TV behind me. The song was so bad that I had no other choice but to turn around and look at it.

'Malaysia, Truly Asia.'

A heavenly picture of an island accompanied the tagline at the end of the ad. I paused for a second and typed 'Malaysia' on my Yahoo search bar. Every picture that popped up was more stunning than the one before. I had twenty articles open about life in Malaysia in a matter of minutes. The more I researched, the more intrigued I became. I finally landed on the main page of a university called Multimedia University. I looked through their bachelor's degree courses and saw a fascinating title: Biomedical Engineering.

'What on earth is that?' I said out loud.

After reading about it for a few minutes, I thought, 'Why not?' and applied. The waiting period was torture, and family members' constant questions about my college plan made it ten times harder. Education was a big thing in Khartoum. Your self-worth was directly tied to it. Being immersed in that environment, I was scared that I would be the failure of the family, the one who didn't make it to college. But even more than that, I was afraid I would be stuck in Khartoum for a long time. The uncertainty was getting to me, and depression was starting to creep in.

A Passion Juncture

One day, I was sipping my morning *Chi be Laban* (milk tea), when my dad put down his newspaper to reach for some cookies. I looked down at the paper, and my eyes caught an ad about a makeup course. I jumped out of my chair, pointing at the newspaper, and said, 'Can I please join this course? It starts in a couple of days. I need to join this course. I am so bored.'

Coming out of the mild shock I gave him when I screamed, my dad looked at the ad for some time and finally replied, 'Be ready by 9 am tomorrow,' before lifting the newspaper to continue reading.

My father parked his car in front of Princess Shahnaz Beauty Academy the next morning. I went inside, so eager to see what this place was like. I browsed through their courses and registered for a Bridal Makeup and Hair course. On my first day, I sat patiently waiting for the course to start. There were twelve other women in the class. Our teacher came in and introduced herself.

'*Sabah Al Khair*, everyone! My name is Vika, and I am your teacher for this class. So happy to have you all!' Vika was short; she had dark skin and silky straight hair that dropped to her lower back in a braid. She spoke softly, with an Indian accent, and had a beautiful baby-blue Saree with beads. Vika had a translator who translated every word she said in the class for those who didn't understand English.

We went on a tour around the academy, and I loved every inch of it. They had different rooms for different classes. They also had a hair and makeup salon open to the public on the ground floor. Time passed quickly that day; we said our goodbyes, and I was already looking forward to Day 2.

The two weeks of the course flew by. I didn't merely enjoy it, I was good at it, too. It was easy for me to master many of the techniques that were taught. A couple of days before the course ended, Vika came to me asking if I could meet with her and the founder of the academy, Ibtesam. We walked to the office, and with a big smile, Ibtesam said, 'Come on In, please.' She wore a colourful Sudanese *toub* that beautifully highlighted her yellow skin and dark black curly hair. She had a massive smile on her face when she said, 'You're probably wondering why I called you here today, so I will jump right to it. Our translator resigned, and we need one as soon as possible to help with the course starting in a couple of days. Vika mentioned that you spoke English very well and suggested that you would be a good candidate to fill that role. Are you interested in working at the academy as our translator?'

I said 'yes' without hesitation. And just like that, I got a job at the academy.

Having my first job was a liberating feeling. In Riyadh, everything had been handed to me on a silver platter. Unable to drive, I relied on others for transportation. I only had to ask if I wanted something. I was thankful for my comfortable life, but I yearned for independence and the chance to prove myself. Landing that job was fulfilling, and it finally gave me the sense of achievement I had been seeking.

My first days as a translator were more challenging than I expected. Delivering the speaker's context in another language required more than a word-to-word translation. But within a few weeks, I got the hang of it, and I also learned about every course they offered. About a month after, I was enjoying my morning coffee at the cafeteria before class started when Vika walked in and sat at my table. We chatted for a few minutes, and then Vika said, 'Olla, I love working with you. You have grown so much in such a short period, and your future will be promising.'

As a person who used to be uncomfortable with compliments, I awkwardly replied, 'Thank you, Vika, for the opportunity and everything you taught me.'

'Olla, I have good and bad news; which one do you want to hear first?'

'Bad.'

'I've resigned from the Academy.'

'What? When? And why?'

'I'm going back home. It's been four years away from my family, and my time here has ended. The good news is that you are more than capable of replacing me. You know all the classes by heart, and I know you will be great.'

It took me a few minutes for all this information to sink in. Vika waited patiently to hear my thoughts; finally, I said, 'This is very unexpected. I don't know what to say.'

'Say Yes. You are right in your element, and I know you will be amazing.'

We hugged, and she went to prepare for the class. I sat for another ten minutes, taking it all in.

'She said I can do this. I can do this,' I kept repeating to myself nervously.

Taking this role was scary. I didn't know if I was ready for it. But something within urged me to take it, despite the fear. After the class, I went to Ibtesam to discuss my new role, and I agreed to take it. Days later, I walked into my very first class as a teacher.

It was hard not to notice the shocked faces when I took centre stage. Fifteen women between the ages of thirty and fifty were sitting, waiting for me to say something. My heart was beating so fast that I worried the women would hear it. Scepticism was written all over their faces. I thought of my mum and tried to channel her confidence and fierceness. I knew my first words would make or break their trust, so I decided to take a risk and crack a joke to address the elephant in the room.

'I bet you never thought that you would be learning from a girl who seems to have just walked out of her mother's womb. But don't let my cuteness fool you, ladies. If you want to know all the secrets of beauty, you are in the right place.' The women laughed, and I could tell the confidence I had faked helped with their decision to give me a chance.

Towards the end of the class, the energy in the room completely shifted. The more knowledge I shared about the topic, the more relaxed the women seemed. The more classes I taught, the more confidence I gained in myself. And with confidence came trust, joy, and fulfillment.

I started to really enjoy the job. Being a teacher made me want to learn everything I could to teach these women, who became a family to me. Their livelihood depended on this course. They hoped to start businesses with the knowledge they were gaining. And I took it to heart. I wanted to give them my all.

As the weeks went by, I grew increasingly grateful for having taken a leap of faith and pursued my passion. It proved that my passion could be more than just a pastime, and I began to shed the notion that the only path to success was through academics. I even started entertaining the thought that if circumstances kept me in Khartoum for longer, I could make a living doing what I loved. The joy it brought would have sustained me until I found a way out.

Three months later, on a calm evening, as I was preparing for bed, my dad walked into my room and said, 'Guess what?'

'You are starting a boy band,' I said sarcastically.

With a big smile, he said, 'Even better. I received your university acceptance letter. You are going to Malaysia!'

From
Kuala
Lumpur

CHAPTER 3

FROM KUALA LUMPUR

'Nothing short of a dream job'

A surge of overwhelming enthusiasm washed over me as I sat by the boarding gate at Khartoum International Airport. I had hand-picked this journey for myself and hoped it was the right decision. Leaving my family behind for a place I had only ever seen in an advertisement was not easy, especially considering how passionate I was about teaching at the academy. But I knew that I couldn't keep myself boxed in. I craved a place to support me in spreading my wings and building a future on my own terms.

Sitting on the metal airport chair next to my only companion—my black cabin bag—I tried to reassure myself. 'No matter what comes out of this,' I thought, 'it will surely be an adventure. And maybe, just maybe, I'll find a place I would call home.'

Twenty hours later, I finally landed at Kuala Lumpur International Airport. I was exhausted and feeling nauseated when I arrived at the immigration line, but the thought of seeing Kuala Lumpur for the first time brought back my excitement. After twenty minutes of waiting in line, I finally made it to passport control. A young officer with a serious face and a dark blue suit decorated with stars and badges sat in an elevated cubicle. He took my passport and flipped it from left to right in confusion, trying to locate the front page, which was on the opposite side from what he was used to. He glanced back and forth between the passport he held in his hand and my face. Finally, he asked, 'What is the purpose of your trip to Malaysia?'

'I came here for university!' I smiled before passing the confirmation letter I held in my hand through the glass window.

'Is there a representative from the university waiting to receive you?'

'Oh, I don't think so. …'

'We can only allow you to enter the country if the university is informed about your arrival. We need to contact the university and wait for a representative to come before we can let you through. Please take a seat, and I will call you when they arrive.'

'Thank you,' I nodded politely, attempting to hide my panic and increased nausea at the thought of waiting for hours (or days) in the airport on my own. I had arrived on a Friday evening, which meant the university was closed. It was the first time in my life that I remember dreading the weekend. The university was three hours away from the airport. So, even if they miraculously found someone right away, I would need to wait about five hours before they arrived.

To distract myself from the long wait, I hunted for a phone to call my parents. My dad picked up, and his cheerful voice travelled from Khartoum to my heart: 'Kuala Lumpur girl!' he said, laughing.

'More like Kuala Lumpur airport girl,' I said sarcastically.

'What do you mean?'

'Well, I need to wait for someone from the university to pick me up. I'm exhausted, Dad. This was such a long trip. I can't wait to lie down in an actual bed.'

'You are almost there. Hang in there.'

Twelve hours later, my name was called. The university representative didn't seem as angry as I thought he would be for having to come on a weekend. On our way to Melaka, where my university was located, I finally understood why my mother had found Dad and me careless with our decisions. The fact that we booked a flight without informing the university and without even booking a place for me to stay was beyond reckless. And because we hadn't notified the university in advance, it wasn't their responsibility to guarantee accommodation for me when I arrived.

Too tired to worry about where I would sleep that night, I passed out in the car for what felt like five minutes, only to open my eyes to see little townhouses disappearing quickly out of sight through the window. I straightened my back and peered closer. Melaka was like nothing I had ever seen before. Enchanted by its cute houses, historical architecture, and street markets, I was no longer tired.

'Maybe it was careless not to do any prior preparations, but it was definitely more thrilling not knowing what to expect …' I remember thinking to myself. There was a strange sense of pleasure in feeling fear and exhilaration simultaneously. It was like jumping into the unknown, clueless about what I would discover on my way down.

We arrived at the university apartment, where a lovely petite Malaysian woman in a colourful headscarf sat at a desk, smiling as we approached. Her smile gave me hope that there was a spot waiting for me. Thank goodness, there was.

Holding the keys to my new home erased all my worries. I went inside my room and smiled at the purple bunk bed. It was my first time seeing one outside of a movie. I dropped my body on the bed and looked at the perfectly arranged houses that decorated my view.

I took a deep breath and whispered, 'Welcome home.'

New Beginnings

The next day was Registration Day. I jumped out of bed and stood in front of my closet, carefully reviewing the nominees for my outfit for my big day. I thought of all the new people I would meet. Although a big part of me was eager, an even more significant part went shy. A sense of anxiety had started to creep in. Being in a new place, not knowing what it would be like or who I would meet, I questioned if I would be able to fit in, make friends … or even like it. My anxiety ignited a strange desire to be as invisible as possible.

That urge helped narrow my outfit options to a loose Kurti-style pink top that completely hid my figure. I paired it with my favourite jeans. Keeping my invisibility goal in mind, I decided to wear light makeup and tie my hair in a simple bun.

Standing in the registration line on campus, I couldn't help but hear voices speaking in the Sudanese dialect. I turned around to sneak a peek, and the speaker's eyes immediately caught mine. From her facial expression, I could tell she also knew I was Sudanese. With a nervous smile, I raised my hand and said hello from a distance. That's how I met my best friend, Sara.

Sara had cheeky eyes, a sharp nose, and a smile that revealed her unevenly arranged teeth. Her smile made her go from bold to super-cute in an instant. She had jet-black hair that was always perfectly styled, complementing her religiously colour-coordinated outfits. Sara was accompanied by her father, who flew with her from the United Arab Emirates to help her settle into a new place in Malaysia. She had been born and raised in the UAE to Sudanese parents. With our similar backgrounds, we instantly connected.

Sara and I spent so much time together exploring our new university life in that first year. I was shy and kept to myself; all I wanted to do was go to my classes and go back to my room. Sara had a different personality. She was social, outgoing, and confident, and she looked for fun everywhere she went. Sara worked hard but partied harder—and I admired that about her. From our first meeting, Sara made it her mission to get me out of what she called my 'extremely boring shell.'

On a Wednesday afternoon, we were having a late lunch with two guys Sara had met on campus. 'So, anything fun happening tonight in the city?' she asked.

'It's ladies' night at Mixx tonight.' They had both replied almost at the same time.

'Oh, let's do that,' Sara said enthusiastically.

'Do what?' I leaned closer to Sara and asked.

'Go to the club, silly! It will be so much fun!' Sara looked at me with her cute smile.

'Sara, I don't want to go to a club; I don't feel like it. I'm tired.' I whispered so the guys wouldn't hear.

'What are you so afraid of? If we don't like it, we will take a taxi and return. Loosen up a little, grandma.'

'Fine. But I'm walking right out if it's dodgy like I imagine it.'

'Deal!' Sara looked straight into my eyes and shook my hand.

A Failed Kidnapping

On our way to the club, I sat, uptight, on my passenger seat, bouncing my right leg up and down. I couldn't shake the discomfort of being in a car with two guys I didn't know. My guard was up. I'd always believed I had no issues with men. Yes, I had had some 'incidents' happen in the past, but I didn't expect them to affect me in any way as a young adult.

Apparently, they had. I was well and truly triggered by sitting in a car with these two 'strangers' who probably wouldn't hurt a fly. Without realizing it, I had trust issues towards men—for obvious reasons.

My mind flashed to memories of Amani.

One of my best friends back in Riyadh, Amani, was invited to lunch by a guy, a friend she met around the time we were home-schooling. Amani was a Lebanese doll I met in High School. She had an adorable baby face, pearl-white skin, and long brown hair.

One weekday, Amani insisted that her sister and I join her for lunch with this new friend. Usually, this would have been an easy 'No, thanks' for me. I was often too lazy to spend my energy entertaining small talk. But on that particular day, I was bored and had no plans, so I agreed to go. Amani sat in front, and her sister and I took the back seat of a fancy black Jaguar. Her friend turned around and greeted us. He had a black cap on, and I could only glimpse his face.

On our way to the restaurant, Amani made an effort to have us all participate in the conversation. But that didn't last long, and eventually, the tunes of Rashid Al Majid playing in the background took over. I watched the streets of Riyadh change. Neighbourhoods started to disappear, and the road turned into a never-ending highway.

I leaned towards Amani's sister and asked softly, 'Why is he taking this road? It looks like we are going out of the city.'

'Oh, you are right. That's weird….' She whispered something to Amani, who looked at the driver and said, 'This is not the way to 'Al Reef Al Lebnani. Why are you taking this road?'

'Oh, don't worry, we are going to a better place.' A sense of fear was evident in his voice. We heard the engine roar as he pressed on the gas, making the car go even faster. The mood instantly shifted in the car, and we all knew something was wrong. I noticed that he kept answering phone calls briefly and shortly like someone was tracking his progress.

'Pull over NOW!' Amani demanded. But the car kept speeding onwards.

I took out my phone and typed to the girls in a text, 'Don't panic, guys. He ought to stop or slow down at some point at a traffic light or a turn. When he does, open the doors and get out.'

At some point, the car started to slow down to take a right turn into what seemed like a residential area with only a few scattered villas in the middle of nowhere. By now, we were at least fifty minutes out of the city.

It didn't take long for us to figure out that he was planning to take us to a secluded villa where many of his male friends were probably waiting. With Riyadh's strict rules on female and male interaction back in the 90s, before the birth of the new Saudi, incidents of this sort were not unheard of. I don't recall ever walking in the street alone there or going anywhere by myself. Even when we walked on the street, fully covered with loose *abaya* and head scarves, we still might encounter verbal harassment. The safest places were the ones dedicated to families only, and that was where we usually hung out.

The car stopped. We signalled to each other, opened the doors, and jumped out from each side. My heart rate accelerated like a bullet train as I saw the ground move beneath me before I jumped. But my feet stood firm on the ground and supported me. I looked around to see if the girls had managed to jump out too. I saw Amani on the ground, but Amani's sister was still inside.

My body stood paralysed for a few seconds as I tried to process the scene. Shocked to see us open the doors and fly out in sync, the guy stopped the car. He opened his door and got out, panicking. From the look on his face, it was clear that he had never done this.

Amani's sister jumped out, and Amani rushed towards him, and commenced pushing and hitting him while screaming, 'What the hell was that? Ah? What were you planning to do?'

We ran over and held her. At this point, he was too scared to do or say anything, which made us more confident. We knew the three of us could kick his ass easily. After an extended pause, he apologized and begged us to return to the car. He promised to take us back to the city.

Any sane person would have punched him in the face for the mere suggestion. But the naïve, foolish young people we were decided he was too frightened to do anything dangerous. His shaky hands made us conclude he wasn't much of a kidnapper! Plus, we were in the middle of nowhere with no means of transportation, and we had lied to our parents about where we were. So getting back in his car was our best option.

He kept his promise, and thank God, we got home safe.

But anything, anything could have happened. I shuddered at the memory as I returned to my current surroundings. Everything is going to be fine, I told myself. Sara smiled at me reassuringly. We eventually arrived at the club, and I was relieved to get out of the car. Mixx Club was different from what I had imagined. It looked like a dark box with a few laser lights shooting into space. There were scattered tables and a riser barely supporting the DJ and his gear. The music blasted so loud that I remember being concerned for the people close to the speakers.

'Can we get a table outdoors? I still need my ears to function tomorrow for class,' I said sarcastically.

I sat on a stool and watched from a distance as people screamed at each other's faces inside the club, trying to have a conversation. I secretly admitted that it wasn't as scary as I thought. As I gazed into this new space, I couldn't help but question the boundaries I had placed on myself. The fear of the unknown, shaped by past experiences and the opinions of others, had been holding me back. But now, with a fresh start and a thirst for adventure, I was determined to break free from these limiting beliefs.

I had embarked on a new life journey; I was eager to embrace all the possibilities. No longer content to live within the confines of my previous life in Riyadh, I was ready to explore the world and challenge myself. This was my chance to grow, to experience life in raw and beautiful forms.

'Maybe Sara is right,' I thought. 'Maybe I am living in a shell of my own creation!'

Heartbreak

It was the end of our first year of university, and it was time to find out our grades for the final exams. Sara and I sat at the Turkish Restaurant we loved on campus. We both acknowledged the tingles in our stomachs. We took a deep breath and logged into the university's online portal. I closed my eyes to recite a quick prayer, interrupted by Sara's scream. I pulled the laptop closer and ran my finger across the screen, desperately looking for my name. I covered my mouth with my palm as I saw the score: 3.75 out of 4.0. We were both on the Dean's List.

'This calls for a celebration. Let's go to KL!' Sara said enthusiastically. 'Let's do it!' We took a three-hour bus ride to the city that same day. Our first stop was Kuala Lumpur's famous Twin Towers, also known as KLCC. We ate, shopped, and walked around the park. Nothing could wipe the smiles from our faces.

'A couple of my friends are going to Nouvo club tonight; let's check it out!' Sara said as she finished the last scoop of the ice cream we'd bought.

Reminding myself that last time it hadn't been as scary as I thought it might be, I went with it. Nouvo was a small club with a darkened dance floor space with live DJs; it had an outside area where people mostly hung out to talk. I wasn't a big fan of the dark or the noise, so I got my Coke Lite and went outside.

'Hey, Girl!' a male voice called from behind Sara. She turned around and gave him a hug. Sara introduced me to Rami, who was a friend of hers. We chatted the night away until it was time to hit the road and return to Melaka. Despite my expectations, it had been an entertaining night.

The following day, I woke up in the afternoon and decided to pamper myself with a big breakfast. While preparing my heavenly omelette, I received a text message from a number I didn't recognise. The message said:

'Hey, Olla, I hope you arrived home safely last night or this morning. Haha. Oh, this is Rami, by the way.' I stopped whisking the eggs to hold my phone with both hands. I couldn't help but smirk as I read the message. Rami was tall, handsome, and stylish. He had an attractive sense of humour. I hadn't given him my number, but I didn't mind that he'd asked around to find out.

After about a week of a lot of back and forth, Rami asked me if he could take me out. We lived in different cities, and he drove for more than an hour to pick me up. I peeked through the window of my room and saw him leaning against his car. I instantly felt butterflies overcrowding my stomach. He looked so sharp in his all-black outfit, which matched his car. It reminded me of how my mum would describe her feeling every time she saw the yellow Volkswagen Beetle.

We had a perfect evening. We spoke for hours and laughed our heads off. Hours felt like minutes with him. It was magical. A year later, we had been talking on the phone constantly and hanging out every chance we got. Although we were yet to exchange the 'three words,' it was no secret that we liked each other. Even the people around us noticed.

During the midterm break of 2007, I spent time with Rami before he travelled to Sudan to see his family. The sensations I experienced watching him leave made me realize the depth of my feelings for him.

'Oh my God, I'm so in love with him,' I remember acknowledging it for the first time out loud. My heart smiled, hearing myself say it freely. Rami was my very first love.

Two weeks passed, and I was holding my phone 24/7 so I wouldn't miss his call when he arrived back in Malaysia. 'He probably extended his stay with his family, and he is just too busy to let me know,' I assured myself with every passing day for the next four weeks.

I ran into a friend at lunch on the first day of the new semester. During our conversation, he randomly said, 'Oh, the other day when I saw Rami in Cyberjaya, he told me. ...'

My hearing, my vision, and my brain went blank. It was like a bomb had dropped, and everything went silent. It took me a few minutes to come back to where I was sitting and make an effort to pretend to listen. 'Oh man, I forgot. I need to run now. Thank you for that chat,' I said. I took my bag and phone and ran to my house. I closed the door of my room and dropped myself into bed.

'He is back? When? Why didn't he call me?'

From that moment on, my mind volunteered to be the lead investigator of the situation. It asked me hundreds of questions a second. When I couldn't answer, it asked me more. When I couldn't bear the confusion any longer, I wondered, 'Shall I call him? Maybe I will call and say "hi." Shall I ask him why he didn't call? No, no, I shouldn't.' Orbiting around the room as I examined these options obsessively, I finally decided to call.

My heart raced as I heard the phone ring on the other end. My steps started to get smaller and faster around the tiny room.

'Hello?'

'Heeeey, hi. How are you?'

'Hey, hey, I'm good. How about you?'

'I'm terrific. Excited about the new semester. How was Sudan?'

We bounced back and forth questions that none of us cared about while desperately trying to ignore the gigantic elephant chilling in the room. We went on with our fake conversation for ten minutes and hung up. My mind and heart were left more confused than they were before calling. A week later, I was emotionally and physically drained, so I decided to let it go and pretend that nothing had happened. My coping mechanism convinced me I should just be happy Rami was back!

As more time passed, it became hard to ignore that things between us had changed. Rami had stopped calling. He never asked me to hang out with him since returning. And when we eventually did speak on the phone again, the fake, superficial conversation continued. For some reason, I couldn't bring myself to ask him what was happening. So I continued to live in mystery. It ate away at me little by little with each passing day.

On a rainy Saturday morning, while Sara and I were having brunch, she asked me if I wanted to go to Zouk that night—the new hot club in KL that everyone went to on Saturdays. My first reaction was to say no, as I wasn't in the mood, but my brain stopped me from replying too soon. Instead, it painted a picture of the possibility of seeing Rami there. So I said, 'Yeah, let's check it out.'

Once we arrived home, my primary mission was to look my best. I started curling my hair and left it hostage to the metal rollers for the next hour. I opened my closet and knew exactly what I would wear; the beautiful off-shoulder baby blue satin midi dress that hugged my curves gently. I had been saving that dress for the day I would see Rami again. I decided my silver stilettos were a good match. I sat at my dressing table and put all my makeup skills to work.

Sara drove us to the club that night. The closer we got, the weirder I acted. My palms were sliding smoothly against one another. My jaw kept grinding out of control. My stomach was rotating in all directions.

Finally, we parked the car in front of Zouk. I took a deep breath, followed by the last mirror check. We walked inside the club, and I felt my lungs bouncing out of my chest from the volume of the music. The club was packed with people. It was dark, and the laser light on psychedelics didn't make it easy to see people's faces. But that didn't stop my eyes from turning into state-of-the-art x-ray machines. They scanned for him everywhere. I spotted his best friend from a distance. My heart sprinted. I knew he was somewhere close. And BINGO! I located him dressed in a slim white shirt and torn jeans.

When I saw him, he turned around and looked directly at me, as if he felt my energy enter the space. As he turned, I saw a girl standing in front of him. I smiled and waved. He turned around and made his way toward us. Pressing my sweaty palms together tightly, I affirmed secretly to myself, 'Stay cool, stay cool, stay cool….' Rami gave me a long-awaited hug.

'I didn't know you guys were coming; good to see you both,' he said casually.

But I knew him too well not to see that he was nervous. He was acting a little awkward too. And then it finally hit me. He'd come here with another girl.

I kept a soft smile on my face so no one could see the disappointment that every inch of my body felt. I couldn't say a single word. I watched Rami make his way back to his date. My lungs gasped for more air, and all I managed to say to Sara was: 'I … I will be right back….' I searched for the closest toilet as if I was being chased. I locked myself in one of the cubicles to give myself time to absorb the shock. I stood there for ten minutes, breathing and negotiating with my tears.

'Pull yourself together. You can do this.'

I took another breath and headed back to where Sara was standing. She was with a bunch of his friends. I intended to fake it until I made it.

I was able to see him from a distance. Laughing, dancing, and having a good time. He didn't seem to be disturbed that I was there at all. I had a million questions racing through my head, all contributing to the one big one: 'WHAT IN THE HELL IS GOING ON??'

When the night was finally over, we made our way back to Melaka. I couldn't speak on the way back. Sara knew what was going on. Neither of us said anything. I lay in bed for hours that night, staring at the ceiling. I was able to hide my feelings in front of everyone, as I always do, and the only release I had was to finally let my tears go, turning my pillow into a tiny puddle. It was the only way I knew to express my emotions.

'Was I being delusional this whole time? Was it all in my head?'

I looked back at our messages. 'Is it possible that I misinterpreted everything he told me?' My brain went on and on in circles until I finally passed out.

The days slipped by, and my dream of a sincere apology phone call grew increasingly distant. I refused to make the first move, determined to maintain a shred of dignity. At the same time, I questioned why it was so hard for me to confront him. I found it really challenging to speak my mind. I felt like I didn't have a voice. Observing Rami with another girl gave me the determination to stay away. And keeping away also meant surrendering to my first heartbreak. Every night, I was consumed by tears. I found solace in junk food but somehow lost weight. I withdrew from socializing with friends and struggled to make it to class, let alone perform well on exams. But by some miracle, I managed to get through it all. The pain was intense, but it was also a wake-up call.

At that young age, I realised that my idealized version of my parents' relationship may have blinded me to the reality of heartbreak. I had built a conviction that Mum and Dad's relationship was how any relationship was destined to end up. Heartbreak was not part of that equation, so it hit twice as hard. Reflecting on the pain, I acknowledged that I may have internalized what my parents had as a necessary ingredient for building a 'home.'

Longing for a sense of belonging, I had unwittingly placed all my hopes on that first relationship—perhaps seeking a home in him. But I soon learned that relying on someone else for my sense of home would only end in heartbreak.

A Leap of Faith

It was graduation day. My parents flew from Sudan to attend the ceremony. They were far more excited to participate in the graduation ceremony than I was. But the happiness on their faces was all the celebration I needed.

Four months before the graduation ceremony, my eagerness for independence had inspired me to accept the first job I found, with an airline company. A couple of days after I signed my contract, in November 2011, I ran into one of my good friends, Thabit. He had gone to my university in Melaka, and we'd always had an effortless connection. We came from similar backgrounds; both born in Saudi to Sudanese parents, we had so much in common.

Thabit was tall and slim, with a nice afro and hip style that reminded me of Bruno Mars. When we both moved out of Melaka, we lost touch. Seeing each other after a few years, we had so much to catch up on. We hunted for a quiet corner in a cafe, and after we caught up with family stuff, I asked him what he was doing for a living.

'Oh my God, Olla, I found the most incredible place. I still can't believe I work there. Trust me, it's not like any company you've heard about. The first time I walked into the office, I was amazed. But what's even better is the people. They come from around the world and are some of the coolest and smartest people I have met.' I nodded enthusiastically for him to continue.

'Do you know the funniest part? I was with a friend who worked for this company when we met the CEO in IKEA, completely by coincidence. My friend told him that I loved the company, and he interviewed me on the spot, and I was hired. In IKEA!'

We both laughed out loud. Thabit's zeal got me totally hooked. 'This place sounds amazing,' I said. 'So what does this company do?' Thabit explained that Mindvalley was about a concept called 'personal growth.'

Until that point in my life, I had never heard the term before. When I asked Thabit to explain personal growth, he translated it into Arabic. I guess he thought I didn't know the words in English, but soon he understood that I didn't know what the term actually *meant*. Thabit was kind enough not to judge and took his time to explain.

'Wow, that sounds interesting,' I said when I finally understood.

'You know, you should apply. You'd be perfect for this,' Thabit said with passion before he took a sip of his Pepsi Twist.

'Thabit, are you serious? You just spent the last ten minutes explaining what personal growth means. How on earth am I perfect for this company? Besides, I just signed a contract for a year. So it's a little too late,' I replied.

'Oh man, you signed a contract? Well, if anything changes, you should keep Mindvalley in mind.'

Three months into my new job at the airline call centre was enough for me to hate everything about it. The schedule was so rough. I had random shifts that switched from evening to morning every three days. Sleeping was a nightmare. My supervisor was rude and treated people like machines. But the worst thing for me was that I needed to get permission for every single move I made—even when I needed to go pee!

As I waited for the next caller to come online, I often found Thabit's words ringing in my ears: 'You know, you should apply. You'd be perfect for this.' The fact that I knew nothing about personal growth ignited the curious little kid in me again. And after I finished my third month at the call centre, I called Thabit and asked, 'What was the name of the company you work for again?'

Mindvalley

Mindvalley, an online education platform for personal growth, was on the rise. When I joined, it had 150+ employees from 40 different countries. Mindvalley's mission was to change education in a way that would improve people's lives. Its strength was its unique way of merging learning, technology, and community while making the entire process fun.

There were many departments within the company, including customer support, design, film, events, marketing, social media, and many more. But the biggest question I had as I browsed their website was how could I contribute? Which team would I join? Thabit asked me to apply and discuss the role with his team, and I agreed.

I had my resume ready, but I needed more. One of the requirements was to create a video cover letter as part of the application process.

This part freaked me out. I felt self-conscious about recording a video praising myself. Where I come from, praising oneself is being arrogant. So selling my 'best qualities' was really challenging. With Thabit's guidance, eventually recorded the video.

While I waited to hear back from them, I spent so much time researching Mindvalley. The more I read, the more I realised that personal growth was a whole world I was yet to discover. I was getting hooked on every new page I read. The company's mission to touch a billion lives, the work culture, the happiness in the workplace—these were ideas I never knew existed. And the sceptic in me was repeatedly asking, 'How are you going to fit in with all of this?'

I didn't have an answer. And that scared me. I was lucky to have Thabit because whenever my comfort zone convinced me that this place was too good for me, he shut that idea down. Within a week of applying, I received an email asking me to come in for an interview. The night before my interview, I lay awake. It was partly because my previous day-night shift had messed up my sleep and partly because I was afraid of not doing well at the interview and being forever stuck in this nightmare of a job.

The following day, my strategy was simple. Look good to feel good. I put on my sky-blue kimono-style dress that flattered my curves; I released my hair from the rollers that held them overnight and went with a natural look using warm makeup colours.

I arrived at the Mindvalley headquarters ten minutes before my interview. I took a few deep breaths and repeated to myself, 'This is it. I got this. I got this.' Then I rang the doorbell. I was greeted by Justyna—a beautiful Polish girl who led the HR department. I took a few steps in, and my eyes couldn't help wandering around, looking at the stunning colours and designs that decorated the space beautifully. Thabit was right; this place was amazing. It was love at first sight.

'Amir is ready for you,' Justyna pointed to the open office door.

In an all-white room, a young gentleman in a black shirt, sunglasses, and familiar features greeted me with a big smile. I was surprised to see that the person behind the desk was a fellow Sudanese, probably in his early twenties.

'Olla, how about we have a casual chat today? No formalities needed; let's talk as two fellow Sudanese people getting to know each other for the first time.' Amir said this in Arabic, with a comforting tone. His words helped me drop the armour I was wearing 'to nail' the interview. I exhaled gratefully.

We chatted for about an hour. Our conversation flowed so naturally and effortlessly. I had not expected to feel this level of comfort talking to someone I was meeting for the first time—at a job interview!

'Thank you for coming, Olla. You've got my green light to move forward to the next stage of the interview process.'

I nodded as I stood up from the white couch and shook his hand. With confidence I had never felt before, I responded, 'Wonderful. Thank you for your time.' It was tough not to bust a 'Can't Touch

This' dance move right there and then. But I managed to hold it inside until I got into the office elevator.

Over the next couple of days, I went through another couple of interviews. The final one was conducted by a lovely Malaysian woman by the name of Grace. She led the customer support team at Mindvalley. While she had this ease and comforting energy about her, for some reason, I lost my cool. I came out of the interview feeling that I had messed it up. I sent a message to Thabit:

'Darling, thank you so much for believing in me and pushing me through this. You were right, this place is incredible, but I messed up my last interview. I'm sad, but everything happens for a reason.'

Thabit wrote back, 'What are you talking about? You got the job, silly!'

A New World

There I was in a completely new world—a new office, new faces, a new job, and a lot of new experiences ahead. It was all so thrilling and terrifying at the same time.

I was happy I had a close friend there to support me through this new experience. But I also knew in my heart that if I made it through the call centre, I could make it through this. As I had no experience in any of the company's departments, I was offered a job as a customer support representative. I had to learn fast if I was going to pass my probation. I needed to learn how to deal with customer inquiries related to their products, use an online education platform, and improve the customer's experience.

My family and friends thought I was crazy to accept a customer-support job after spending six years doing a biomedical engineering degree. They questioned why I didn't pursue a career in my field, but for me, it was all about curiosity. With an engineering degree, I knew what a job in that field would entail. During my final year of university, I trained at the Kuala Lumpur Hospital and understood the scope of work in that field. However, the opportunity to work at Mindvalley was a new and exciting challenge that I couldn't pass up. I was unsure of what I was getting myself into. But it reminded me of the cluelessness I felt when I transferred to the English high schools in Riyadh. Everyone thought I was crazy back then too. But if it hadn't been for that first crazy decision, I would not have been going through this experience. That thought made me wonder where I would end up after *this* decision.

In my first week at Mindvalley, I was too shy to speak up. I was intimidated by the fact that most of the people in the office spoke English as a first language. Even those who spoke English as their second language were fluent. At that point, I was able to converse and understand the language very well. I was just less articulate than everyone else.

And everyone sounded so bright. I often left meetings wondering how on earth I had got that job!

To add to my frustration, my initial encounter with Vishen, the vision-ary Founder and CEO of Mindvalley, fell short of my expectations.

Hailing from Malaysia, Vishen exuded a charismatic aura with his meticulously spiked black hair, captivating eyes that mirrored his unwavering passion, and a playful demeanour that eschewed conventional formalities. Despite his youthful years, Vishen had already established a remarkable track record of entrepreneurial success, earning admiration and inspiring countless individuals with his profound mission and steadfast values.

During my induction at the office's living space, I coincidentally met Vishen as he passed by. Until that moment, my only exposure to him had been through YouTube videos. As he caught sight of me, he swiftly pivoted and strode purposefully in my direction. Vishen had a commanding presence when he walked, seemingly proclaiming, 'I am changing the world; you just watch me!' His sudden approach caught me off guard, and panic began to set in.

With a warm smile, Vishen extended his arm and greeted me, saying, 'You must be Olla. It's a pleasure to meet you.' In response, all that escaped my lips was a jumbled phrase, 'Abah laba ha,' a language I never knew I spoke. Following that awkward exchange, I couldn't shake the feeling that the CEO of Mindvalley might have formed an unfavourable impression of my intelligence.

The feeling of being the dumbest one in the room was not fun. I wanted to catch up, fast. One of the tools that helped me learn English quickly was the discipline I had shown every day after school with Dad. So, daily, after work, I would go over email updates from the team and try to figure out the parts I couldn't understand. Google was my lifesaver. I would also listen to the Mindvalley courses to familiarize myself with the content. Slowly, I understood the updates my teammates were giving at team meetings. I stayed late at the office and helped out with any project I could get my hands on, to learn new skills.

While doing so, I faced a more significant challenge—that of expressing myself. Coming from a conservative culture that idealizes perfection and doesn't encourage questioning, expressing, or making mistakes, it was hard for me to speak my mind without judging myself. I struggled to share ideas without deeming them unimportant. I struggled to use phrases like 'I don't know' or 'I don't understand' without feeling stupid. While the team continued to recognise my professional progress, I received constant feedback that I was too quiet, and that I spoke too softly for anyone to understand what I was trying to say. It was embarrassing.

Daily meetings became a nerve-racking experience. I was pushing myself to speak more often. I would prepare talking points and practice them in advance. But every time it was my turn to speak, I would rush through it like a bullet train, so that I would only have to talk for as short a time as possible. My frustration levels with myself kept increasing, and my suspicions that I wasn't as smart as everyone else kept growing.

The one thing that kept me holding on was my boss, Hannah, a Venezuelan badass who was intelligent, expressive, confident, and cheeky. She had a giant smile, deer eyes, fair skin, dark black hair, and prominent cheekbones. I admired how Hannah expressed her thoughts so freely and unapologetically. At the same time, she was a good listener and a fantastic problem solver. But what stood out to me the most was that she was a compassionate leader.

Hannah saw beyond the introverted shell I was hiding in. From day one, she saw something I couldn't see in myself. She kept highlighting my triumphs and accomplishments, no matter how small or insignificant they may have been. She created a space that made me feel safe and welcome every time we spoke. Yet, despite all her efforts, it took me almost a year to lower my walls and be myself around Hannah. Slowly, I started to show her my vulnerable side and express my fears and challenges.

As I attended meetings with different teams, I saw how people were comfortable expressing themselves, asking lots of questions, and admitting if they didn't know the answers or had made a mistake. So I started to practice. Every time I used phrases like 'I don't know' or 'I don't understand,' I felt lighter. Whenever I dared to admit a mistake, I realised nobody was coming for me with pitchforks. Before I joined Mindvalley, I had never even recognised that I had an ingrained belief that I needed to do everything right—or wrong things would happen. It was an 'Aha' moment to conclude that the less 'criminal' I felt being vulnerable, the less self-punishment I imposed, too.

My fearful programming was very robust, and it took work to undo. I had to peel off one layer at a time. The more time I spent at Mindvalley, the easier it became to express myself and not feel judged by it. Every time I took a step towards being vulnerable, I found that I was growing faster, both personally and professionally. So I kept taking those steps every chance I could.

The Journey Continues

It had been five years since I moved to Kuala Lumpur. I loved everything about my life there. I loved how affordable it was to have a comfortable lifestyle. I loved having a beautiful apartment with a swimming pool and a gym. I loved the endless variety of cuisines in the city. I loved the abundance of massages and the spas that decorated KL's every corner. But what I loved most was the celebration of all holidays, from Christmas to Chinese New Year to Eid Al Fitr. I was celebrating my holidays and everyone else's. It was wonderful.

The day I found out that I was eligible to bypass immigration and use the smart e-gate at the airport I genuinely believed I'd found home. I no longer felt like a foreigner in someone else's country. That inspired me to look into getting permanent residency in Malaysia. But the most common response I received when I looked into citizenship was, 'Ah, don't waste your time. In Malaysia, you'll never get it.'

I also heard, 'I know a friend married to a Malaysian guy and has kids AND was denied citizenship!' or 'No one knows how the process works here. It's a mess.'

To say it was discouraging would be an understatement. But I wanted to pursue it anyway. I didn't want to accept that someone else's story would be my own before I even tried. But the more I inquired, the more hopeless it all felt. I did take the permanent residency point-system test, which uses many questions to rank your profile and determine eligibility for permanent residency. My results were far from the benchmark!

I then looked at the 'Malaysia: My Second Home' program for foreign nationals to get a ten-year renewable visa. It was all going well until I read the criteria to enrol:

Show proof of liquid assets of MYR 500,000.

Upon approval, place a fixed deposit in any local bank of MYR 300,000.

So that was out!

Finally, I discovered the Talent Pass, a program giving professional workers a ten-year renewable visa. Its criteria seemed a lot more attainable than the other options. The only one I couldn't meet was the minimum salary. It was twice as much as I was making at the time. So I set a goal to get there within the next two years—maximum.

A year later, I was coming back to Kuala Lumpur from a trip abroad. Glancing at the long immigration queue, I thanked God for the empty e-gates. I scanned my passport but kept getting an error message. I went to another e-gate, assuming that the one I tried was having a bad day. But I still couldn't get through. I went to the immigration officer right next to the gate.

'I'm trying to use the e-gate, but for some strange reason, it's giving me an error message.'

With a poker face, he scanned my passport and said, 'Now, Sudan can't use the e-gate. You have to go through normal immigration.'

'Is there a reason for that? I've used it for the past several years.'

'Sudan has been banned from the e-gate due to yellow fever until further notice.' He stamped my passport and gave it back to me.

As I turned away and made my way towards baggage claim, it felt as though someone had punched me right in the heart. It wasn't the inconvenience of not being able to use the e-gate that caused this feeling, but rather the realization that my hopes of finally finding a place to call home had been snatched away just as I was beginning to entertain that thought. It had been a small step, but it felt significant, and now it was gone.

My salary hit the benchmark a year later, and I applied for the TalentPass. I was more desperate than ever to become a permanent resident of Malaysia. I believed I had finally found a place to call home.

Two months later, my application was rejected without justification. I didn't even know how to feel that day. It was as if my emotions were numb. I remember that I went straight to sleep after I got the news. I was mentally tired.

When I opened my eyes the following day, my first thought was, 'If Kuala Lumpur doesn't have space for me, there must be a place on this earth that does. I just need to find it.'

It wasn't the first time I had experienced being in this situation. I was sad, but I wasn't shattered. Getting a rejection meant that this place wasn't meant for me, nor was I meant for it. I just needed to keep believing and keep going.

A Dream Job

With the start of a new year, I was ready for bigger challenges at work. I still had my employment visa, so I didn't need to leave Kuala Lumpur just yet. I decided to focus on work. By that time, I had examined all the departments in Mindvalley, and I was clear about what excited me and what didn't spark any interest. The team I admired most was Events. The Events team was a collection of super-talented women who organized some incredible transformational events at exotic locations around the world. Their job was to design experiences, travel the world, meet exciting individuals, transform lives—and get paid for it. I found that to be nothing short of a dream job.

Of course, everyone on that team had years of professional experience in the event industry. How would I fit in with my, yet again, zero experience? On a calm and cosy Sunday, I came across a tiny blue notebook with an attached lock and key that I had been given a while back. I took it to the balcony along with my hot tea. I opened the first page and wrote, 'I am now part of the events team. I'm handling projects that I'm so passionate about. I love my new team. We communicate so well, and we love working and playing together. I'm a vital member of the team. I demonstrate confidence, knowledge, and leadership in everything I do. I love all the travel opportunities and the new friends I'm making around the world. I am so happy with my role on the events team.'

One of the concepts I learned in my first year at Mindvalley was manifestation, a tool to make my goals become a reality using visualization and affirmations. Writing in detail about what it is that I really wanted would help in the process of making it happen. The trick was to register it as though it had already happened. Why not give it a try?

A couple of months later, as my eyes were glued to one of my customer service projects Hannah came in with a big smile and stood in front of me. I slowly removed my headphones and looked at her with a sarcastic and scared expression.

'What did I do now?' I smirked.

'Well, my darling, you just manifested your dream job. The Events team just approached me and asked if they can offer a job for you to join the team. Do you want to go ahead with the interview?'

I stood up slowly with both my palms covering my mouth.

'NO?'

Laughing, Hannah hugged me and walked away saying, 'Congrats, babe. Watch out for the interview invitation.'

Hannah was the only person I had dared to share this dream with because she was always supportive and encouraging. But as soon as I received the interview invitation, I panicked. Thoughts were flying in from every corner of my mind.

'Man, I have just gotten out of the "I don't feel so dumb" zone. I don't know if I am ready to feel dumb again.'

'I don't even know if they will select me, anyway. I have zero experience.'

'I am usually shy; how will I handle events with big crowds?'

I had all of these crippling thoughts dragging me down. But somehow, my heart was fighting back hard. I wanted this so badly. I felt conflicting emotions of fear and excitement. Back in the house, I took out the blue notebook beside my bed to get peace of mind. I unlocked it and drew a line in the middle of the next blank page. On the right side, I wrote, 'What's the worst thing that could happen if I go through the interview and don't get it?' On the left, I wrote, 'What's the best thing that can happen if I go through the interview and get the job?'

The worst thing that could happen if I messed up the interview was that I would stay at my current job. Nothing would change. But I realised that the best thing that could happen was that I would be part of the dream team. I would learn from the best, travel the world, meet interesting people, and design epic experiences.

The decision was easy, then. I needed to focus and hope for the best. So, I took a leap of faith again! I passed the interview, and just like that, I made it to the team. My first exciting project was an event called Awesomeness Fest which was taking place in the Dominican Republic.

I couldn't quite process it when I heard that I would be going there. The Dominican Republic was the sort of place I thought I'd only ever see on TV!

To get there I needed a visa. There was no Dominican Republic embassy in Kuala Lumpur, but I was told that getting a US visa would be sufficient to gain access to the border. A good friend of mine from the office was also attending the event and needed a permit. She was Malaysian. So we filled out the US visa application online and scheduled our visa interviews the same day.

At 8 am on a Thursday, my friend and I were seated in the waiting area of the US embassy, anxiously waiting for our numbers to be called. Hers came first, and I wished her luck. Soon I saw my number on the screen. I took a deep breath and walked towards the interview booth. An American guy who looked to be in his forties smiled as I walked in. He lifted my passport and asked why I wanted to visit the US, and I responded. All of a sudden, his questions shifted in a lot of other directions unrelated to my business trip:

'So, where is your father now?'

'What does he do for a living?'

'Where is your mother?'

'Why did you study engineering?'

After about ten minutes, he gave me back my passport and said that I wasn't qualified for this visa. I took my passport and walked to the exit area, where my friend was wearing a big smile. From my facial expression, she quickly understood that things hadn't gone as well for me. I told her I would take the rest of the day off and went home.

I sat in the back of a taxi, feeling deeply sad about losing the opportunity to go on this trip. It hadn't crossed my mind that my visa would be rejected, given that I was going for business. My friend and I had the same qualifications. We carried the same letters, worked for the same company, and had the same intentions.

The only difference was where we were born.

I cringed at the thought of sharing the news with my new team. I felt embarrassed to say that I wasn't given a visa because of my passport. My dismay instantly deepened as I felt a familiar and very profound sense of rejection. Being in Mindvalley for the past two years, working and hanging out with people of all nationalities, I had forgotten about this feeling. But at that moment, it came back tenfold.

Eventually, I informed the team that I wouldn't be attending and they should find a replacement. That really sucked. With the fire I felt inside, I decided this time I wasn't going to feel sorry for myself or drown in self-pity. Instead, I pulled out my notebook and wrote, 'Today, I commit to making travelling the world part of my life regardless of obstacles or circumstances. I set the intention to travel to four new countries every year.'

A couple of days later, Tanya Lopez scheduled a lunch meeting to discuss my roles as part of the team. Tanya, the head of Mindvalley

Events, was an outstanding American Colombian whom I admired. She was intelligent, confident, and possessed a vibrant and strong personality that you would feel when she walked into a room. Our conversation felt light and casual, which helped me be myself. At the same time, I was terrified about the whole visa situation and whether it would be a problem for me to move forward with the team. Tanya eventually addressed the big fat elephant in the room.

'You know I'm concerned with the whole visa situation. We travel a lot, and I would hate it if you were left behind and did not get to experience being on the ground with the team....'

Tanya had a valid concern. No other team members had this issue, as they were from Europe and the US. They were able to travel without applying for visas most of the time. On the other hand, I needed to apply for a visa for almost every country in the world, including the country of my birth.

'Honestly, Tanya, I don't know what other countries' visa situations will be. But I promise you that I will find a way, and I will travel to every country we need to visit. There will be a way.'

I don't know where the illogical optimism I had back then came from. But Tanya believed it, and so did I. I just knew in my heart that I wouldn't give up on my dream that easily. Thankfully, I was able to keep my job and keep my dream.

From Puerto Vallarta

CHAPTER 4

FROM PUERTO VALLARTA

'De-attach my self-worth'

With five months remaining until the upcoming event, I eagerly anticipated the new destination; Puerto Vallarta, Mexico.

Amidst the excitement of the destination, I was growing anxious about facing yet another visa denial. It wasn't merely the fear of missing out but the worry that another rejection would jeopardize my job.

If I continued encountering travel difficulties, it would inevitably affect the entire team. With one less member at each event, the strain on the team's productivity would become unsustainable in the long run. Despite my uncertainties about the visa situation, I consciously tried to conceal any concerns in front of my teammates. I didn't want to amplify my own doubts and worries.

Realizing the need for a backup plan if my initial attempt didn't succeed, I resolved not to give up quickly this time. Firstly, I had to navigate the process of obtaining a visa for Mexico. Once that was sorted, I had to find the most convenient route to Puerto Vallarta. Fortunately, I discovered a Mexican Embassy in my city, which initially brought relief. However, that was short-lived when I realised that my passport was expiring, and the only way to renew it was by returning to Sudan.

Blessing in Disguise

The moment I laid eyes on my dad's beaming smile at the airport terminal in Khartoum, I knew instantly that the arduous 15-hour journey had been entirely worthwhile. Being able to reunite with my family before embarking on my first work adventure was a blessing in itself. On the day of my arrival, I woke up in the guest room of my parent's house at 4 am, still struggling with jet lag. Before my mind could fully grasp my surroundings, the delightful scent of Sudanese Bakhoor wafted through the air, instantly enveloping me in a familiar and comforting embrace.

Stepping out of bed, I made my way into the spacious white kitchen. With a warm cup of coffee in hand, I settled myself at the kitchen table, opening my laptop to tackle the day's tasks. As I scanned my emails, I realised it was still too early for my brain to fully engage in work mode. Instead, I embarked on a different mission—locating the Mexican Embassy in Khartoum. Navigating their website, I diligently searched for valuable information regarding visa applications.

Soon, a spark of inspiration ignited, prompting me to research the US Embassy in Khartoum. A brilliant idea emerged: 'What if I applied for a US visa here rather than in Malaysia?' Perhaps the interviewers who live among Sudanese people would see each applicant as an individual rather than perceiving everyone as immigrants trying to escape. In a matter of minutes, I completed the online application form and secured an appointment for the following day. I was pleasantly surprised by the swiftness of the process, especially in comparison to my experiences in Kuala Lumpur.

I wanted to apply for a US visa because I wanted to be able to fly through the US with my teammates. I also knew that getting the US visa stamp on my passport would make obtaining other visas easier in the future.

At six in the morning, my father arose for his Fajr prayer. The sound of typing on the keyboard must have piqued his curiosity, drawing him toward it. With his customary warm smile, he inquired, 'The jet lag hit hard, huh?'

'Oh yes. It sure did! But, Dad, guess what? I just applied for my US visa, and my interview is tomorrow!' I exclaimed, unable to contain my excitement and nerves as I covered my mouth with my palms.

'Very good. Very good,' my father responded, his approval evident in the familiar English phrase he reserved for when he fully supported the plan.

The night before the interview, sleep eluded me. I ran through countless potential questions the interviewer might ask. Yet, amidst my racing thoughts, I kept reminding myself, 'Just be confident. That's all.' My interview was at 8 am. I got up at 6:30 am and made my way to the prayer mat. I performed Fajr and remained on my mat with my eyes closed, reciting a silent prayer to God. As we made our way to the embassy, my father recited a few short prayers that he always says before embarking on his own journey to work. Only this time, he was reciting them for me.

About fifteen minutes later, we were in front of the embassy. Dad conveyed his best wishes and waved me off. Inside the interview area were four open booths without doors, allowing one to overhear the entire conversations of applicants. Only a handful of people were waiting their turn. My name was called after ten minutes.

I took a deep breath and walked over to the booth. The interviewer, an African-American man in his thirties, greeted me warmly. 'Good morning, Olla!' He said as I stepped into the booth. 'What is the purpose of your trip to the United States?'

Striving to exude confidence, I explained the purpose of my journey and shared information about Mindvalley. He turned to the computer screen before him as I spoke, typing away. I could discern from his keystrokes that he was searching for Mindvalley. 'That's a great start!' I secretly thought to myself.

The fact that the interviewer focused on my job and documents instead of delving into personal matters like my mother's whereabouts put me at ease. I continued discussing the upcoming event, sharing details about our plans and the anticipated number of attendees, barely pausing for a breath.

Suddenly, he opened my passport and remarked, 'But I don't see any trips you have made so far with this company.'

'That is true,' I replied, maintaining my composure. 'I needed to prove my capabilities before being allowed to travel. This is my first chance to demonstrate to the team that I am capable of handling travel responsibilities as well.'

Kindly, he looked at me and said, 'Your visa is approved. Please proceed to make the payment.' My heart soared. I thanked him and walked away in shock. I reached the exit door, my jaw still hanging open, when the guard noticed my bewildered expression. 'How did it go?' he asked. I looked at him, still barely blinking, and said, 'I got it!'

Smiling back, he said: 'You must have read Yasin (A chapter in the Quran we use as a prayer to ease a challenge ahead) this morning. Congrats.'

I laughed because I had! I sprinted towards the car, where my dad patiently waited, faking a sombre expression. In an instant, his face transformed as he caught sight of me. Anticipating the perfect moment, I paused for a few heartbeats before shouting, 'I got it, I got it!' as I literally jumped for joy.

Dad's smile came back as he exclaimed cheerfully '*Ya Salam, Alhmdullah*!', which translates to 'That's wonderful, thank the Lord!'

This small moment of victory had a deeper meaning for me. I felt immense relief because it gave me this instant verification that I could indeed travel the world. I took it as a sign from God to keep going on the path I'd chosen. It validated my belief that if there's a will, there's always a way.

Everything Changed

After securing the American visa stamp in my passport, obtaining other visas became significantly easier. Although not mandatory for entry into Mexico, I decided to acquire the visa anyway. Surprisingly, it was granted to me on the spot. It seemed that, at long last, my fortune had taken a turn for the better.

As the aircraft prepared for its descent into the United States, the flight attendants distributed small slips of paper to passengers bearing the words 'US Customs and Border Protection.' My heart quickened its pace, its rhythm resonating with anticipation as the prospect of crossing immigration loomed. Despite holding a valid US visa, a nagging unease persisted within me. Seeking solace, I quietly recited a prayer.

To my pleasant surprise, the immigration officer proved far from intimidating. He appeared to be in his early thirties, a friendly white American who efficiently processed my entry upon sighting my visa. A similar seamless experience awaited me in Mexico. It was a breeze! Arriving in Puerto Vallarta served as a catalyst, awakening my senses to the boundless possibilities that lay before me as I embarked on my global exploration.

'The more I see of the world, the faster I will find my place in it. My life will never be the same again,' I remember thinking.

Heaven on Earth

The shimmering sun cast a mesmerizing glow upon the limitless ocean. The meditative sounds of the sea gently caressed the pristine white sand. Lush palm trees adorned the island. And the tropical beats playing from the cascade of swimming pools competed with the birds that sang in the morning. Each time I gazed out my window, it felt like I was peering into a tranquil screensaver on my computer.

Unable to resist, I closed my eyes and inhaled deeply, savouring every precious moment.

Adding to the allure, the resort offered an all-inclusive experience, granting me the freedom to stroll into any restaurant and indulge in whatever culinary delight I desired without the need to check the price tag. It was an unprecedented experience I had never encountered nor fathomed before.

But what I anticipated the most was the extraordinary array of events we were about to embark on. Months of meticulous planning and preparation were about to unfold before our eager eyes. The breathtaking excursions, the out-of-this-world costume parties, the deep connections, and the transformative sessions—everything we had envisioned was about to materialize.

Every morning for ten days, I embraced the tranquillity of the early hours. I would step onto the balcony with a towel, ready to engage in prayer, meditation, and morning yoga. Sitting in peaceful meditation for fifteen minutes, I would inhale the crisp, fresh air and let the heavenly sounds serenade my senses.

These moments were essential for preparing me, not just for my role as an organizer, but also for the inevitable self-doubts that would arise from taking on this challenge. I was still fairly new to this whole 'event organizing' world, and I was standing with some of the best women in the game. So I needed to make sure I didn't let fear take the wheel; I needed to be in charge of my responsibilities, and my emotions, at all times.

I shared a room in Puerto Vallarta with my colleague and dear Estonian friend, Kristi. She embodied joy and ease, exuding a lively spirit, and I cherished our time together as roommates. However, I hadn't anticipated the internal struggle I would face in revealing parts of myself that she wouldn't typically see!

As the event approached and the intensity and pressure mounted, I strongly wanted to ground myself through prayer. Yet, a sense of shyness and mild embarrassment held me back from expressing my faith in front of Kristi. Knowing she was an atheist, I worried she might pass judgment, feel uncomfortable, or perhaps both

Most of the time, I managed to wait until she left the room to offer my prayers. It made me discover how unconsciously I was adjusting my identity to fit in, a tool I had learned growing up in a multicultural environment in Riyadh. But I felt a deep desire to pray at the very moment she was doing some work on her bed.

What would she perceive if I covered my head and humbly touched the ground with my forehead? Would she feel uneasy or find it odd? These questions swirled in my mind, fuelling an internal debate. Amidst my contemplation, my friend announced her intention to take a shower. As soon as she closed the bathroom door, I sprang out of bed, ensuring the blinds shielded my actions from prying eyes outside. Carefully, I placed a towel on the floor, serving as my make-shift prayer mat. Swiftly, I offered my prayers, mindful of the limited time, before returning to my position on the bed.

It was an eye-opening experience for me. I never thought I would feel self-conscious to be myself in front of a friend. It dawned on me that the pervasive media coverage of Islamophobia in Western countries had subtly influenced me. Unconsciously, I harboured a fear of being judged or even subjected to potential hostility.

This was one of many instances when I caught myself hiding a part of who I am to blend in. I believed covering up the unique parts of my identity would make others feel more comfortable around me and thus like me more. But what I didn't comprehend back then was that I was doing this at the cost of showing up to the world with my fully expressed self. The younger me didn't know that it wasn't my job to make someone else comfortable with who I am; my primary job was to be comfortable with … me.

The event ended! The number of emotions I went through in just ten days was unbelievable, from intense excitement to stress, to happiness, to gratitude, to insecurity to happiness again. A true rollercoaster of emotions. In this short period, I gained more self-awareness and insights about my new role than I could have ever acquired in a year confined to a desk! I felt blessed to have been given the opportunity to immerse myself in this event in Mexico. It truly was what I would have imagined heaven on earth to be like.

The Other Side of the Coin

After concluding the event, I had a week to explore Mexico, and an intriguing thought crossed my mind … 'Does Mexico feel like it could be a place I could call home one day?'

I acknowledged that finding a conclusive answer within such a brief timeframe would be challenging. To truly understand the essence of daily life in Mexico, I need more time to be immersed in its culture. Nevertheless, being on the opposite side of the world sparked my curiosity. I made a personal promise that whenever I ventured into a new country, I would pose the same question, recognising that the answer would gradually unveil itself. Asking this simple yet profound question felt like a tribute to the journey I was undertaking.

After a week of exploring, it was time to go back. Although I was only transiting in Houston, I still needed to go through immigration there. A white man in his fifties sat behind the glass with a very serious face on. He flipped through my passport.

'What is the purpose of your trip to the United States?'

'I'm just on my way back from a business trip I had in Mexico.'

'Have you ever been arrested by an officer before?'

'I'm sorry?' I genuinely thought I hadn't heard him correctly.

'Have you ever been arrested by an immigration officer before?'

My facial expressions instantly changed at the ridiculous question. 'No, I have not.'

'Well, the system shows me that you have been arrested by an immigration officer before. Please follow me.'

The officer led me to a crowded room filled with around fifty individuals, primarily Asians, Arabs, Africans, and Latinos. Numerous officers sat in cubicles, calling out travellers' names and inquiring about their travel history. Eventually, my name was called, and a female officer stood behind a glass window and asked me a series of routine questions, such as 'What do you do?', 'Where do you live?' and 'What is your salary?' She perused my passport before returning it to me. However, she made no mention of my purported arrest, which I knew to be a fabricated story that the officer had concocted to subject me to additional screening. I deduced this was due to the type of passport I possessed, rather than anything he had seen on his system.

I eventually got through the border, but little did I know that this incident wasn't going to be the last of its kind. The more I travelled, the less I knew what to expect at the border of every new country I visited. Among them all, Hong Kong proved to be the worst. Despite meticulously submitting countless documents in advance to establish my credibility as a law-abiding individual, the process was far from smooth. After waiting two weeks for my visa to be approved, I thought the hard work was done. Needless to say, I was wrong.

When I reached the immigration counter in Hong Kong, I was asked to step out of the queue and follow an officer to a room. I waited for hours, completely clueless as to what was going on. When I insisted on being told what I was waiting for, the officer finally said, 'We are waiting for the police investigator. He will be here shortly to investigate you.'

It was hard not to feel offended, angry, powerless, and humiliated at the same time. I was released after three hours. I was only visiting for the weekend!

It is astonishing how this whole system works. The people who are required to obtain a visa before their arrival in any country have to prove that they are trustworthy before they are permitted to enter. This means going to the embassy, going for interviews, paying for an application, and submitting piles of documents—verified bank statements, health insurance, letters from employers, payslips, etc., etc.

Yet, the people who go through this intensive vetting process before arrival are always the *very ones* who are stopped for further questioning and screening. Those with the privilege of travelling visa-free, who haven't gone through any sort of background checks, always cross immigration the fastest. That always baffles me.

As my travel went from twice a year to up to six times a year, I began to encounter all types of comments and questions at the border. The differences were amusing.

> *Bangkok* – 'Please come with me for further questioning.'
> *Lisbon* – 'Sudan, wow, this is a good passport!'
> *Maldives* – 'Fill the paper slip and go back to the back of the line'
> *Montego Bay* – 'What's up, sister?'
> *Zanzibar* – 'I am learning Arabic'

Guanacaste – 'We can't let you through.'
Rio de Janeiro – 'You look Brazilian.'
Atlanta – 'Have you stolen anything before?'
Tokyo – 'Welcome to Japan!'

Navigating border crossings was always an unpredictable experience for me. One moment, I would be greeted as a welcomed visitor, and the next, viewed with suspicion as a potential threat. These unexpected encounters during my travels only heightened my desire to travelled alone. Dealing with longer waits at counters or being subjected to additional inspections was one thing, but having someone wait for me while I endured these ordeals felt degrading.! The worst part was the well-intentioned sympathy I received from my Western friends. One sentence, in particular, would send a chill down my spine and drain the blood from my heart, 'Oh, I never knew how privileged I was to travel around the world without ever checking if I needed a visa until I heard about what happened to you on the last trip.'

I hated that. The sympathy enforced the idea that I was somehow less than others and needed to be felt sorry for. It made me feel like a victim and stripped me of my power. This is not to say the experiences I went through were not indeed unpleasant or that they did make me feel small, insignificant, and unworthy. An encounter like the one I had in Atlanta when an officer asked me, 'Have you stolen anything before?' burned like a flaming ball in my chest and continued for days after it happened. It took me a while to shake off the insult of this assumption that I was some sort of a criminal because of where I came from (despite all the evidence of my career). Moments like these made me resent myself sometimes. Yet, pity wasn't the emotion I needed to get me through such occurrences—what I needed was encouragement.

Not only did I get pity from my Western friends, I also got the same reaction from people who'd gone through the same struggles. First, they would express their shock at the fact that I was travelling so much. Then, they would reaffirm our 'bad luck' and our victimhood.

For all these reasons, I made the decision to travel solo as much as I could. At the same time, an interesting thing was happening: the more humiliating situations I faced, the more self-respect I gained once I'd overcome the pain of the incident. I began to de-attach my self-worth from these incidents. Gradually, I came to realise that these occurrences were not a reflection of my worth. In truth, they held little correlation with my identity. I began perceiving that the officers, who exuded disdain through their words or actions toward those they deemed inferior, were perpetuating a cycle that mirrored how they felt toward themselves. As I passed their judgmental gaze, a series of remarkable encounters, extraordinary individuals, and a cocoon of affection surrounded me, regardless of their endorsement. I started to believe that these experiences had to be part of my journey—they gave me no choice but to love myself more.

The more I accepted who I was, the less reactive I became when someone hit me with condescending words or attitudes. I always reminded myself of what was important, which was to make it to my destination just as everyone else would—regardless of what I needed to do in the process. My journeys were uncertain, but there was one thing I was sure about, I had the same right as everyone else to see this planet. And I was not about to let a piece of paper dictate otherwise.

Lo and behold, that piece of paper called my passport was about to get me deported!

From
Dubrovnik

CHAPTER 5

FROM DUBROVNIK

'The gateway to my inner world'

It had been four years since I delved into the fascinating world of personal growth. Before joining Mindvalley, I had yet to fully realize the extent to which our surroundings can shape our daily habits and behaviour. Once I began working there, immersed among people who lived and breathed personal growth, I couldn't help but catch the vibe.

At Mindvalley, personal growth wasn't just a buzzword, it was a lifestyle. Everywhere I looked, I saw people embracing healthy mental and physical habits. Even meditation, which back then was considered 'woo-woo,' was a customary practice, complete with its very own meditation room. Junk food was rare, and working out was a common pastime. Conversations flowed effortlessly from manifestation to self-actualization, without anyone batting an eye.

But it wasn't just talk. The company also offered various classes led by employees, from yoga to dance to breathwork. I started with meditation and yoga, and before I knew it, I was hooked, so much so that I created my own morning routine, one that has become sacred to me. Each morning, my routine began at 6 am with a sacred ritual: prayer, yoga, and meditation. That simple practice has transformed me in ways I could never have imagined. My negative self-talk has lessened, and I commence each day with a calm mind. It all started with subtle adjustments, almost imperceptible at first. But over time, these incremental changes accumulated, setting off a chain reaction that reverberated throughout every aspect of my life. The profound impact of these seemingly small shifts astounded me, forever reminding me of the immense power hidden within even the tiniest steps.

Getting Hypnotized

In 2015, I jetted off to the stunning city of Dubrovnik for an event we were organizing. And it was love at first sight. The ancient city walls, the sparkling Adriatic Sea, and the serene atmosphere all combined to make Dubrovnik the most enchanting place I've ever been.

On the first morning of the event, I spread out a towel on the balcony, fired up my phone, and, using a special app, found the Qibla to pray towards Mecca. Wrapped in a blanket like a giant headscarf, I closed my eyes and let the serene atmosphere wash over me. After prayer, I stretched into some yoga poses to wake up my body and get into the right mindset. I meditated, visualizing myself confident and relaxed, with a big smile on my face, as the team cheered me on.

That day we had parallel workshops occurring. I was assigned to support the room where Marisa Peer was doing a hypnotherapy class. Marisa had three decades of experience as a therapist and was named Britain's Number One therapist at the time. I was thrilled to be assigned to her room; I was a big fan and couldn't wait to see her in action.

Toward the end of the session, Marisa announced she would be hypnotizing the group. Since help was not needed at that point, I decided to give it a shot. Marisa passed around pieces of paper, inviting us to write down our goals for the hypnosis. And since I was there on a whim, I jotted down the first thought that came to mind: 'I want to express myself freely, to speak my mind no matter how many people are in the room.'

You see, speaking up in groups has always been a challenge for me. I never understood why I felt so paralysed, especially since I was a chatterbox around my friends and felt perfectly comfortable in one-on-one conversations. But put me in a room with people I didn't know well, and I'd shut down. I hoped to overcome that fear. It was beyond my awareness that even deeper fears lurked beneath the surface.

As Marisa initiated the hypnosis session, she encouraged us to close our eyes, inviting us to embrace the awaited tranquillity. My restless thoughts initially resisted, but her soothing voice gently persuaded me to surrender. I sensed her delicate touch as she tenderly retrieved the paper from my grasp. With her guidance, we were instructed to shift our gaze upwards as if peering toward our eyebrows. In this poised position, we lingered for a few moments before being beckoned to gently close our eyes again. Enveloped in the soothing ambiance she created, Marisa skilfully navigated us through a visualization technique that transcended ordinary boundaries. Gradually, I was transported away from the confines of the room, the presence of others, and the weight of my various roles and responsibilities. All that remained was the resounding echo of Marisa's voice, ushering me into a state of deeper relaxation.

At one point, Marisa asked us to imagine three scenes from our past, present, or future. 'Just allow whatever needs to come,' she said.

I was amazed at the vividness of the images that flooded my mind. It was as if I were truly experiencing them in real-time. The first scene was my dad and I sitting on the roof of our house in Khartoum. The image brought a warm sensation to my body, reminding me of the comforting feeling he always gave me. The second scene was of myself and the male cleaner in the bathroom. I felt my lungs gasp for air. My body started to feel uneasy, and I felt my palms getting sweaty.

Marisa asked that we picture the third scene, but I was stuck on my second. I tried to switch my mind away from what I just saw, but it was hard to follow any more instructions. Anxiety was building, so I opened my eyes slowly and then closed them again. I listened to the session, though I was not consciously participating.

Marisa continued for about ten more minutes. She asked us to reflect on why those particular images came to us. 'What are they trying to tell you?' She asked.

We came to the end of the session. I took a deep breath, opened my eyes, and got off the chair to help Marisa wrap up the class.

Whenever we had a break that day, I found myself contemplating the session and the scenes. Deep down, I knew these things were not random recalls from the past. They were indeed trying to tell me something.

I wanted to find out what it was, yet I was not a big fan of the idea of going back to these memories. I wanted them to be done and gone. But the session clarified that those memories were neither—instead, they were just stashed away somewhere in my mind. In the years I studied personal growth, I often heard how important it was to deal with emotions instead of accumulating them. I knew I needed to gather the courage to look into what had been buried in my mind and discover why I was afraid to look back. I took out the blue notebook and wrote, 'Today, I start my healing journey.'

Although uncertain of the nature of my healing or the path to follow, I just knew I needed to start by confronting emotions I was afraid to face. I believed if there was fear, then something needed to heal.

Facing My Past

Following the hypnosis session, I added journaling to my morning ritual. With numerous accounts attesting to its benefits, I believed that putting pen to paper would help me untangle my thoughts and understand them better.

My approach to journaling was simple. Each morning, I would awaken and allow my thoughts to flow freely onto the pages without constraint. In the evenings, my focus shifted to delving into subjects related to emotional healing through research. These two activities became cornerstones of my daily routine. Although lacking a strict structure, I trusted my intuition to guide me along this journey. While researching, I stumbled upon the timeless saying, 'When the student is ready, the teacher will appear.' This powerful phrase reminded me to persevere in my quest, confident that the answers I sought would manifest when the time was right.

One evening, as I engaged in my usual research on Google, a book title seized my attention: *You Can Heal Your Life* by Louise Hay. To my delight, I discovered it was a free eBook online. From the first few pages, I found it increasingly difficult to tear myself away. The more I immersed myself in Hay's words, the greater my curiosity grew about the author herself. Louise Hay, a renowned emotional healing and personal growth figure, captivated me. In the 1970s, she dedicated her life to assisting individuals with terminal illnesses in overcoming their conditions through her developed techniques. Her battle with cancer and subsequent healing journey further fuelled my fascination with her remarkable story.

I watched tons of videos of her seminars and interviews; her words resonated with me deeply when she shared that every illness is rooted in a 'dis-ease' within the body. She believed unresolved negative emotions could accumulate over time and manifest as physical ailments. The idea that emotions and the body are intertwined was a concept I couldn't ignore.

The notion that something from my past could potentially harm my body frightened me, so I continued reading. Louise put forth a

compelling argument: we can significantly diminish the likeli-
hood of physical ailments by addressing our emotional traumas and
releasing negative emotions. True healing, she maintained, neces-
sitates diving deep into our minds and uncovering the underlying
origins of our dis-eases.

This was a life-altering realization. I became acutely aware of the
profound connection between my mental state and physical well-
being. It was both intimidating and empowering to comprehend the
impact my thoughts could have on my overall health. I also found
a morning and evening meditation program created by Louise Hay,
specifically designed to rewire negative thoughts and beliefs. Eager
to take charge of my well-being, I faithfully listened to these medi-
tations for six months. Additionally, I incorporated the practice of
reciting affirmations, another tool recommended by Louise Hay,
focusing on two areas: releasing the past and finding my voice.

My journaling took a remarkable turn as I went deeper into my subconscious. Memories long forgotten began resurfacing, demanding
my attention. One morning, after a meditation session that momen-
tarily took me away from the external world, I found myself lost
in the rhythm of my breath. As I sat in silence, a surge of thoughts
flooded my mind. Hastily, I reached for my notebook, eager to capture every insight. The burning question that plagued me for months
surfaced again: 'Why did I witness those specific images during the
hypnosis?' The answers flooded my consciousness so intensely that
I had to write furiously to keep pace. The sheer magnitude of the
revelations left me stunned. It became clear that the memory of the
cleaner in the bathroom, which had emerged during the hypnosis session aimed at conquering my fear of speaking up, was not a

random recollection; It was a direct response to my ongoing struggle to find my voice. This insight was a profound one for me.

Following that harassment, I summoned the courage to reach out for help, only to be met with disappointment. I felt unheard and unsupported instead of the guidance and protection I longed for. It was a pivotal moment that left an indelible mark on my teenage self, leading me to believe that my thoughts and opinions held no significance to those around me. The aftermath of this experience manifested as a constant struggle to express myself, share my ideas, and engage actively. Speaking up became daunting, reserved only for those I held closest and trusted implicitly.

Journaling about this experience unearthed the underlying cause of my difficulty speaking up—and gave me a newfound compassion for my younger self. Whenever I hesitated to share a thought or an idea, I pictured the teenager who felt unheard and lonely: I wanted to give her more love instead of dismissing her. This shift in my perspective profoundly impacted my healing and overall well-being; I felt lighter and more at peace with that part of myself.

I continued to journal, meditate, and listen to more videos and lectures on emotional healing from past traumas. I also discovered other excellent teachers, like Wayne Dyer. His book *Wishes Fulfilled* became one of my favourites. I listened to all of his talks that were available online. I replayed my favourite videos to the point that I could recite them!

I discovered and experimented with different tools—chakra healing, tapping, and energy healing. I kept using practices that resonated with me and discarded what didn't. Gradually, I started to feel different. I felt more energetic, experiencing more moments of calm, and felt less trapped in my head.

These changes were beginning to reflect in my professional life too. I was more motivated, focused, and productive at work. I also felt less intimidated to voice my ideas and opinions. My efforts were recognised, and I was entrusted with important projects, which was an external affirmation that I was on the right track. As I immersed myself deeper, I explored other modalities beyond books and lectures. I experienced the healing powers of sound therapy, float tanks, electric acupuncture, and essential oils. I also tried more intense practices like breathwork, which left a lasting impression on me.

My first breathwork session was held in a dimly lit room with about twenty of us. We were invited to recline on mats arranged in a circular formation on the floor. At the centre of the circle stood a man dressed in loose white clothes, playing a unique musical instrument—later, I identified it as a hang drum. I found a mat and lay down, surrounded by candlelight.

We closed our eyes and were told by the guide to follow his breathing directives. It began with slow, calming breaths, and I soon became entranced by the soothing music and the peace I felt in my body with each inhalation. The fragrance of lavender floated towards me, and I realised that a facilitator was walking around with essential oils, bringing them close for us to enjoy.

My body was at ease, allowing my mind to let go and not be disturbed by extraneous thoughts. The guide's breathing instructions changed, and the pace quickened to a point where breathing became harsh. It was so fast that I began to sweat, and I felt my limbs become so heavy that I couldn't move them. I had the strange feeling that I would lose a body part if I did. But the guide urged us to push on: 'Don't stop. You are getting out of your comfort zone, and emotions will come up. Don't be afraid. You are letting go of what you don't need. Keep breathing.'

I was scared by the unfamiliar feelings that arose, but I persevered. I felt tears wash down my face. With every teardrop, I felt an emotional release. My breathing slowed, and I regained some sensation in my limbs. We were asked to remain in position for a while before emerging from the session.

The peace I felt after was indescribable. I was at ease, free of thoughts and worries. That session sparked my interest in trying other breathwork sessions worldwide.

Utilising the tools I had acquired became more than just a means to an end or a quest for a particular outcome; it became an integral part of my life. I realised that growth is an ongoing journey, and this toolkit became my trusted companion, helping me navigate the rhythm and flow of life's challenges.

I also learned that no particular toolkit would provide any shortcuts. Healing was not a destination; it was a process. At every stage, the right tool presented itself. I just needed to trust and go with the flow.

Most importantly, Dubtovnik served as the portal to my inner realm—the realm of my mind—a territory I had seldom explored and whose profound influence and potential I had underestimated.

My thoughts emerged as the potent architects of my mind, sculpting my emotions and consequently shaping my actions and surroundings. If my mind held the remarkable ability to craft my very reality, it stood to reason that it played an integral role in my quest to unearth a true home. Could the journey to find home necessitate its inception within my mind—Do I need to find a home within my mind to ultimately manifest itself in the world around me?

That's when I knew that Dubrovnik marked the beginning of a significant journey—the journey of finding a home within my mind.

From Miami

CHAPTER 6
From Miami

'The embrace of a stranger'

Over the course of five years, I embarked on a journey that took me across the globe. During this time, I was privileged to visit eighteen countries and twenty-five cities. From the enchanting towns of Europe to the vibrant streets of Asia, the bustling metropolises of the United States, and the unique splendour of Africa, I was truly blessed to witness the world's incredible diversity. Despite encountering inconveniences along the way, my passion for traveling never dwindled. I faced challenges mainly at the borders or when applying for a visa. However, Once I successfully navigated through immigration, a world of boundless exploration unfolded before me, allowing me to freely wander within the country's borders and sometimes venture into neighbouring nations.

I cherished the stamps on my passport, not just for their aesthetic appeal but for their convenience in obtaining visas. I frequently travelled for work, but thanks to my job's remote work policy, I also had the flexibility to work from different cities when I craved a change of scenery. And during my vacations, I checked off several countries from my bucket list. Whether I travelled with friends or colleagues or ventured alone, each experience left me yearning for more. The more I saw of this planet, the more I wanted to see … more!

My next stop was Guanacaste, Costa Rica. Another place on earth I was thrilled at the prospect of discovering. This time, I had my partner in crime, Kadi, by my side. She joined Mindvalley around the same time I did, and we've been thick as thieves ever since. With her long, golden locks cascading down her back, stunning green eyes, and a smile that could light up the darkest of rooms, Kadi proves that mermaids exist (minus the tail, of course!). Her beauty, both inside and out, is otherworldly!

Normally, I avoid travelling with others, but the thought of a 30+ hour trip to Costa Rica made me reconsider. With a journey that long, I knew we were in for a wild ride!

There wasn't a Costa Rican embassy in Kuala Lumpur, but after some research, I learned that a valid US visa was enough to grant me access to the border. Miami was the transit hub we chose on our way to Guanacaste. Growing up watching all the Hollywood movies filmed in Miami made it climb the list of my top cities to visit in the US.

After a long 23-hour trip, we finally made it to Miami. The exhaustion disappeared as soon as the airport taxi drove us across the city. All those images I grew up seeing were in front of my eyes, and I couldn't help but sing out loud:

Party in the city where the heat is on,

All night, on the beach till the break of dawn,

'Welcome to Miami!

Bienvenidos a Miami!'

Since this was a quick transit, we decided to make the most out of our short stay. We dropped our bags at the hotel and headed straight to South Beach to honour the song we had been singing since we arrived. We walked all over the city, discovering every street we could. When night fell, we met with some friends for dinner. Although that dinner was the last stop we'd planned for that day, our friends insisted that we hang out for a bit more and experience the nightlife in Miami.

Our flight to Guanacaste was at 5 am the next day, so we planned to explore the night with our friends for only an hour or two before heading back to the hotel to get some rest. But of course, that didn't happen! That plan failed so miserably that at the end of the night, we had to ask the taxi driver to take us to the hotel and wait outside. We threw some of our stuff back in the suitcase and headed straight to the airport. Luckily, we made it right before the check-in counter closed. At the boarding gate, we laughed desperately at how exhausted we were from the crazy day we'd had. Yet, we were proud of having made the most out of our time in Miami.

Two flights and about ten hours later, we made it to Guanacaste. Feeling too tired to walk to immigration, the thought of the beautiful 5-star resort awaiting us gave us just enough energy to take on this final part of the journey.

At the immigration line, Kadi passed through, and I was right behind her. The young male officer flipped through my passport from left to right, trying to locate my visa. He finally found the US visa stamp and scanned the details. After a few minutes of staring at the sticker, he finally said in an adorable accent, 'Can you wait for a minute, please? I will be back.'

He left his cubicle holding my passport and went to the neighbouring officer. The young gentlemen returned and asked me to go to the next counter to talk to the immigration head officer. 'Oh, God,' I thought to myself.

I felt in my gut that something was not right.

My Worst Nightmare

The minute I saw the head officer's face, I knew I was in trouble. She had sharp features, sleek black hair pulled back in a bun, and a poker face that hadn't seemed to have smiled in a long time. She looked at me and said the words of my worst nightmare, 'You don't have the right visa; we must send you back.'

I felt my stomach fall to my feet as soon as she finished that sentence. Stuttering, I managed to push these words out of my mouth, 'What, what do you mean? I have a US visa and was informed that it was sufficient to cross the border.'

With a sharp tone, she replied without making eye contact, 'We only accept multiple entry visas, but you have only two entries. The airline will take you back to the country you came from.'

She handed back the passport to me. I desperately tried to change her mind. 'Ma'am, please, the two entries allow me to go back and forth to the US, which is what I need for transit. I used this type of visa when I entered Mexico and other neighbouring countries. I am here for a business trip, and my colleague is right there. You can contact the venue that we are working with. I came from so far away, and this is a crucial business trip.'

Nothing I said helped. The officer was adamant. So when all failed, I asked, 'Can I at least speak with my friend who's worried and doesn't know what is going on?'

Escorted by an officer, I walked to Kadi on the other side of the border, looking terrified. She rushed towards me. 'What's going on? Why aren't they letting you through? What's happening?'

'Babe, they said I don't have the right visa, and they are sending me back to the US. I don't want you to worry about me. Let the team know that I will find a way to come back before the event starts. I will let you guys know as soon as I land.'

With teary eyes, Kadi asked: 'But where are they taking you?'

'They are taking me back to Miami. I won't be too far. I will come back.'

As I sat in my seat and the flight took off, it all started to sink in. My emotions danced between fear, guilt, rejection, and embarrassment. I had no idea what awaited me. I was scared!

I landed at Miami airport at 2 am. The immigration officer asked how long I was planning to stay. That straightforward question made me break down in tears. I had no more strength, both mentally and physically. Weeping, I told the officer what had just happened and that my plans were all up in the air.

As a Sudanese passport holder, I had not been issued a multiple-entry visa to the US. Instead, I was granted the two entries I needed to transit for my trip to Costa Rica. But when I was sent back, I lost one.

The immigration officer, upon hearing my situation, kindly granted me an additional entry on the chance that I would eventually reach Costa Rica. This act of compassion instilled a glimmer of hope within me, reassuring me that things might still work out. I went to the baggage claim to pick up my suitcase and watched as every single bag got picked up by its owner, except mine. Frustratingly, I learned at the lost-baggage counter that my suitcase was still in Costa Rica. Despite being assured at the Costa Rican border that my bag would be placed on the same flight, it had failed to reach me.

So besides my handbag and the clothes I had on, I had nothing.

The airport lacked Wi-Fi, and I didn't have international roaming on my phone to contact anyone for assistance. By the time I exited the baggage claim, it was already 3 am, and to make matters worse, all the shops and restaurants at the airport were closed. After enduring six flights spanning over forty hours of travel without any sleep, the word 'exhausted' couldn't adequately capture the extent of my weariness.

I made my way on foot from the airport to the taxi stand, desperately seeking refuge at the nearest hotel that would accommodate a late check-in. Within ten minutes, I arrived at a sketchy-looking motel. The check-in counter resembled a caged cubicle manned by an intimidating figure with a prominent scar on his face. I reassured myself that it would only be a few hours before I could relocate to a proper hotel.

I went to the room, locked the door, and dropped myself onto the bed. I gently moved the blanket to slip underneath it. To my horror, the entire bed was crawling with tiny black bugs. I jumped out, screaming. I looked around the room in desperation.

'Okay, okay, there's a couch. I will sleep on the couch,' I said loudly and rushed towards it. I examined the stained, beige, old-fashioned couch. The same bugs were swarming all over it. I stood still in the middle of the room, unable to process what was happening. I felt utterly helpless. I was on the verge of a breakdown. But I stopped my mind from going there. I needed every ounce of my energy left to get through that night, which was not over yet.

I took a deep breath, grabbed my handbag, and left the room. The guy at the front desk frightened me so much that I didn't bother asking for the $78 I'd paid for the room. I returned to the main street, praying for a taxi to pass. I didn't even know where I was planning to go. I just knew I couldn't stay in that place any longer. Thankfully, a taxi came by. I jumped up and down, waving my hands in the air as though I were on a desert island signalling to a helicopter.

'Can you take me to the airport, please?'

'Yes, ma'am.'

Despite my exhaustion, I couldn't sleep just yet. Instead, I aimlessly wandered through the airport, unsure of what I was searching for. Out of nowhere, I saw a solitary figure standing in a small booth. I squinted, questioning if it was a product of my imagination. Astonishingly, the person remained the only one in sight at four in the morning.

Intrigued, I approached the booth cautiously, my gaze fixed on the booth. As I drew nearer, I gasped to discover that it was a lady selling SIM cards. I bought the overpriced SIM card without hesitation and swiftly searched for hotels. Amid my research, I paused to look back: both the woman and the booth were still there. Nevertheless, I believed in my heart that she was an angel sent by God.

I found a hotel that would allow me to check in that early. I entered the room, threw everything on the floor, and passed out.

Waking up the following day to a hundred messages from my team, my CEO, and people who'd heard about what happened, I felt an instant sadness at the realization that it was not all a bad dream. After responding to everyone to let them know that I was okay, I sat on my bed, wondering what I should do next.

The Unexpected Plan B

Jane, a warm-hearted Mexican woman in her 50s, greeted me at the gate of her humble house, where she lived with her son. She rented an extra bedroom out to tourists to make ends meet. Opting for an Airbnb seemed practical while I grappled with my visa predicament. Jane kindly offered a brief tour of the house, revealing a collection of miscellaneous items all over the place ranging from guitars to bicycles and assorted odds and ends. At that moment, I realised I should have thoroughly reviewed the listing's photos before making my reservation. Nevertheless, my mind was preoccupied with weightier matters that demanded my attention.

She then took me to my room. It was small, barely fitting a queen bed and a small table. But since I didn't have luggage, that space was fine. Over tea, I told Jane my story and why I needed a place so urgently. Sympathetic, she offered to drive me to the Costa Rican embassy the next day.

When we arrived there the next morning, I said, 'Jane, thank you so much for driving me here. I'm sure you are busy, so I will get a taxi back home once I am done.'

'Nonsense, I'm coming inside with you, and I will wait for you for as long as needed.'

At the embassy, I discussed my case with the administration officer to examine my options for returning to Costa Rica. And sadly, the options were … nil. As a tourist in the US, I was not eligible to apply for a visa without residency. My last glimmer of hope was mercilessly shattered. And it hit me like a tonne of bricks: 'I am missing the event I have been working on for a year, and there's nothing I can do about it.'

While I was internally grappling with this reality, Jane keenly observed the helplessness across my face. With utmost compassion, she enveloped me in her arms and said, 'I am so sorry, darling.'

It seemed unfathomable that a single letter on my visa specifying the number of allowed entries could completely disrupt and dismantle my meticulously planned trip! I frantically revisited the embassy's website in search of any overlooked requirements, but to no avail. What's even more bewildering is that even the airline, responsible for ensuring passengers have all the necessary documents prior to boarding, seemed unaware of this seemingly insignificant rule!

I broke the news to my team, and their response was overwhelming with an outpouring of love and support. Their primary concern wasn't the event itself but rather my well-being. They urged me to stay in Miami, allowing me to be in a similar time zone and provide online support to the best of my abilities. Their genuine desire was for me to feel connected to the event, a sentiment I cherished deeply!

For the next few days, I supported online. Every time I was able to resolve customer issues or figure out technical problems they couldn't fix, it made me feel less guilty for not being there in person. And when I wasn't supporting the team, I stayed in my room.

A part of me felt left behind and unworthy. The other part wanted to understand why this had happened to me. 'Am I equal to everyone else when everyone is there, and I am here in some random Airbnb?',

'Do I even deserve to be part of these experiences?' These were the sort of questions that haunted me.

Occasionally, my thoughts took a better direction—'What is this experience trying to teach me?'—yet with every day that passed in my tiny room in Miami, I felt myself falling into a deeper, darker psychological hole. One morning, as I was lying on the bed with my laptop, I heard a knock on the door.

'Olla, are you there?'

'Come on in, Jane.'

'My dear, you barely ate, talked, or even left the room for the past couple of days. I know what happened makes you sad, but you are in Miami and need to take advantage of that. We are going to the beach, and I will take you for a nice dinner—Miami style. And I won't take no for an answer.'

I smiled and said, 'Yes, ma'am.'

As I stood at the water's edge, witnessing the gentle embrace of the ocean's waves upon my feet, an overwhelming urge to pray consumed me. With closed eyes, I directed my thoughts to the divine. Silently I recited, 'Dear God, please grant me the strength to accept what has transpired. Help me embrace the pain, releasing the burden of anger, blame, and frustration. Please grant me the courage to take responsibility and rise above this setback. I trust that there is a purpose behind guiding me to Miami instead of Guanacaste, and I humbly request that you reveal it to me.'

With my eyes still closed, I became aware of the chirping of the birds, the scent of the ocean breeze, and the soft sand beneath my skin. At that moment, I felt like my prayer had been answered.

A surge of gratitude welled up within me for the countless angels who had supported me throughout this experience—my dedicated team, dear friends, the compassionate US immigration officer, the SIM card vendor, my loving family, and even the attendees of the event who had sent messages of encouragement. And above all, Jane.

I realised that my focus had been fixated on what had gone wrong, inadvertently overshadowing the abundance of love and compassion surrounding me. This realization prompted me to question the validity of my self-perception as rejected and unwanted.

Contemplating further, I pondered … 'Is it possible that in my toughest experiences of rejection, I am also being showered with unconditional love that I have failed to see? What if being welcomed is not determined by visas but by the embrace of a stranger?'

These questions allowed me to see that I had also been given acceptance and love whenever I faced rejection. I felt a shift within me, a deep desire to flip a switch in my mind—to take control despite the circumstances. I may not have possessed the power to alter the moment the officer decided to send me back, but I could harness that very moment as a catalyst for personal evolution, stretching the boundaries of my mind, body, and soul.

I grew to understand that these situations unfolded to reveal the love and compassion that consistently showed up in my life. Each of these instances was a reminder, urging me to delve into gratitude for the boundless love that surrounded me wherever I went.

Through this experience, I also came to a profound understanding of the remarkable power of compassion and kindness. Even the most minor acts of kindness can create a sense of belonging and connection, making individuals feel part of something greater than themselves. This sense of belonging is not confined to a specific physical location; it can be as simple as a heartfelt embrace from a stranger.

This realisation has ignited within me a recognition of my own tremendous capacity to make a positive impact. I now comprehend that extending a helping hand or offering a kind word can make someone feel profoundly valued and loved. This awareness has liberated me from the limitations of a victim mindset and has empowered me to aspire to embrace a role as a compassionate individual.

Miami has done more than flip a switch within me, guiding me to perceive the love that emerged amidst challenges and redirecting my focus away from rejection. It also prompted a profound contemplation: if the embrace of a stranger could evoke a genuine sense of belonging, could I potentially discover my own sense of home through an alternative path?

From Rio

CHAPTER 7

FROM RIO

'Choosing love over fear'

It was almost six in the evening, and my brain began to fry. I was ready to call it a day at the office and go home. As I wrapped the cord of my laptop charger around itself in preparation to pack my things, Ronan, a colleague who sat across from my desk, approached me with a sweet smile.

'Hey, Olla! Do you have a minute? I want to talk to you about a project related to events.'

'Sure, let's do it,' I responded, tired but curious about the project.

Ronan was a cute Brazilian with fair skin, small sweet eyes, and hair that reached halfway down his back. He was one of the new hires that year, and we hadn't spoken much since he joined the company, but he seemed to have a soothing and loving energy. For the next couple of weeks, we worked on a project together. On one of the

final days, Ronan had to work late to finalize it. To thank him for
his efforts, I offered to treat him to lunch the next day.

Shortly after arriving at the restaurant, we found ourselves deep into
a very deep conversation. We shared some very intimate stories about
our lives without knowing how we got there. I told him about incidents I had never shared with anyone before. Ronan mirrored my
vulnerability and shared some of his secrets too.

Two hours passed like a flash, and after that lunch, we felt that we
had built a bond. We began to spend more time together after work.
Sushi, shisha, and shawarma were our go-to pleasures.

As I got to know Ronan better, my admiration for him grew. His
presence was refreshing, and being around him felt effortless. He
possessed qualities that I truly admired—he was easy-going, funny,
considerate, and brimming with energy. Surprisingly, we connected
on a deep level despite our initial differences. I had perceived him
as having a loud Brazilian personality, contrasting with my reserved
nature. Yet, our connection was undeniable, and it was so easy for us
to be around one another.

As our friendship grew over the months, our bond became
incredibly strong. It was evident that Ronan had developed feelings for me beyond friendship, and I found myself reciprocating
those sentiments. However, I was hesitant to pursue anything
beyond friendship. I was content with how things were in our
relationship and did not actively seek a romantic involvement. I
cherished our connection and didn't want to risk complicating or
jeopardising it.

One day, we explored a new place for shisha. While drawing on the strawberry mint-flavoured shisha, we started sharing our past relationships. We talked about our experiences and our fears when it came to dating again. 'I am afraid I cannot trust again after I gave everything to that relationship and got ghosted. I really don't know if I have it in me anymore,' I opened up to Ronan.

'I understand. It is not easy. I also get scared when I feel things are getting serious. I always freak out and jeopardise the relationship because I am afraid I will get hurt. I want to be in a beautiful relationship with someone I care about, but I don't want to mess it up,' Ronan said.

'You are an amazing person, Ronan. Truly. If you trust yourself, you won't mess it up.'

We looked at each other. Ronan leaned in for a kiss. Unconsciously, I pushed him away.

Stunned, he had nothing to say.

'Ronan, I honestly think you are amazing. And I do like you; I don't want to ruin what we have. Let's stay friends.'

He respected my decision, and our friendship remained unchanged. I admired the fact that he treated me no differently after that evening. On the contrary, he was more loving and caring. That in itself made me like him a little bit more. For months, Ronan and I continued to hang out. He was there for me through it all; whenever I needed help, he was there. When I was bored, he was there. When I had a bad day, Ronan was there. He became one of the people closest to me.

After a year, my heart finally gave in to the kindness, sweetness, and authenticity that Ronan demonstrated with every interaction.

Knowing Ronan for a year had eased my hesitations about taking our friendship to a deeper level. I was fearful, but I decided to do things differently this time. I professed that I wouldn't worry about the future or have any expectations. All I wanted was to be present with the joy I felt every time I was with him.

Of course, that was an almost impossible job for my analytical mind. It constantly reminded me about what was being left unaddressed—that Ronan hailed from a completely different part of the world, one with other cultures, faiths, and beliefs. A part of me questioned whether I should pursue this relationship, knowing the complications we might face down the road. Yet it was too early to think of all that. So I decided to enjoy the moment and cross those bridges when I came to them.

Back to Basics

As time flew by, Ronan and I celebrated our second anniversary as a couple. Our relationship was unlike anything I had ever experienced. It was characterized by light-heartedness, transparency, and an abundance of joy. We were so in sync that disagreements were rare, and being together felt second nature.

At the end of that year, my parents were preparing to visit me. It was our newly created ritual, that we would spend the end of the year together. 'I want to meet your parents!' Ronan said with enthusiasm on one of our dinner dates. I almost spat out the food I was chewing.

When it came to my romantic relationships, I usually chose to keep them to myself unless the relationship reached a stage that required my parents' involvement. My parents had no problems with me dating. The problem was that if I shared with them that I *was* dating, they would not stop asking when we planned to get married. That sort of pressure I didn't need.

'Hmm, that is sweet, babe, but maybe we should do that next time,' I said to Ronan. 'I don't think it's a good idea for you to meet them so soon.' I took the next bite of my falafel, hoping he would let it go without further questioning.

'Meu Amor, I know you are probably worried about introducing a Brazilian to your family, but if we don't do it now, we will never do it. It's not the most comfortable thing, but I want to start heading in that direction.'

'Honey, being Brazilian is the least of my worries ... your tattoos and earrings are what terrify me!' We both laughed. 'On a serious note, babe, you don't understand.' I continued, 'If I introduce you to them, it means that we are super serious, and they will keep asking me what our next steps are and yada yada yada. Let's not worry about this for the time being.'

'I'm curious, if we were to take the next biggest step, like if I want to marry you, what do I need to do?'

The way he casually threw out this question made me want to laugh and cry simultaneously. But I took it as a piece of curiosity on his part, not as an actual proposal.

'Well, the cultural aspect is … interesting. First, in Islam, I should marry someone of the same religion. Otherwise, the person will need to convert. So for you to marry me, the first step is conversion.'

I thought that would put him off. But he replied, 'Well, I knew it would be something like that. I come from a Christian home, so I have some experience with these things and respect the customs. So, are you really religious yourself?' Ronan asked.

'Since moving from home, I have never lost my connection to my faith. I am connected to it in a way that makes sense for who I am and my life without needing to define if I am a religious, a modern Muslim, or the other hundred names to describe it. I will never ask you to convert to any faith for whatever reason. That is why I never wanted to bring this up.'

I sighed.

'You know, babe, Islam is a big part of your life that I don't know anything about. I want to know about that part of your life, too. Learning about your faith will help me know you more, and I want to know you more. I would love to learn about it. Can you teach me?'

That response reflected the kind of person he is. Someone who sees life with eyes of love, not fear. It made me want to learn to see life the same way.

'I don't know if I am the best person to teach you, but you know what? I have always wanted to go back and study the basics all over again. Why don't we learn together?'

'I would love that!' Ronan said with excitement.

For the next couple of weeks, we started to study the basics of Islam together. We would randomly choose a topic and learn about it twice a week. We went from learning the five pillars of Islam to looking at some of the histories, to reading simple verses of the Quran. One day, we stumbled upon a program titled 'Meditation in Islam— Rediscovering the Spirituality of Islam.' The personal growth maniacs in us purchased the online course immediately.

We went through every module together: Spirituality, Peace, Surrender, and Transcendence. Every time we completed a chapter, we would discuss what we'd learned and share our opinions on it. Taking that course was one of the most beautiful experiences. Seeing the direct connection between everything I have learned in personal growth and the religion I grew up with was so transformative.

The process made me realize that when we are born into a religion or culture, sometimes, we blindly follow what we were told while missing all the richness and wisdom of it. Ronan and I kept digging and learning. The more we researched, the more we connected the dots of how similar it was to what we had been learning in personal growth: the affirmations, the meditation, the fasting, the gratitude—they were the same practices, only taught differently. This learning journey was as eye-opening for me as it was for Ronan. The beauty was that we were able to tailor it to our unique needs and preferences, making it an enjoyable and light-hearted experience.

We kept it between ourselves, which allowed us to explore and learn without the interference of outside opinions or unsolicited advice. This freedom from external pressures made our journey all the more meaningful and rewarding, allowing us to truly immerse ourselves in the experience and gain valuable insights. Sharing it with Ronan was profound, and our bond became even more potent.

Meeting the Folks

On a Wednesday morning, I managed to get my mum all to myself. To ensure unbiased reactions, I chose to speak with her and my dad separately.

'Mum, there's something I want to share with you….' I dreaded opening my mouth, and I resented her reaction before it even happened.

'*Khair, Inshallah*! (May God bring only the good!) Is it about your future groom?'

I laughed at the typical cheesy Sudanese phrase. 'Hmm, something of that sort, I guess! I have been seeing someone for two years. He works with me in the company and is an amazing guy. He insisted on meeting you guys while you were here.'

'And he has been curious to learn about our culture and religion.' I knew I needed to drop that sooner than later.

'What do you mean? Why? Where is he from?'

'He is Brazilian.'

'Interesting. So you are following your brother's footsteps by bringing us someone we can't communicate with, ha?' Mum jokingly referred to my Turkish sister-in-law, who communicates with my mum in sign language. 'I look forward to meeting him,' she concluded before going back to answer her WhatsApp messages.

Wait, what? I never expected my mother to be so chilled out. For a moment, I questioned if she had registered the information I shared, but when she continued to be in a good mood throughout the day, I figured that she was indeed okay with it. My dad had a very similar reaction to the news, but honestly, I wasn't worried about him at all. He had always been the least dramatic of the family, which made it easy to bring up things of this sort with him.

I picked up my phone and dialled Ronan's number, grinning like a lunatic. I told him about my parent's reaction. That day, we were on cloud nine! This exchange made me recognise that as I had been changing and growing, so had my parents. As we matured, our relationship had evolved as well.

On a Friday, we made plans for dinner at a charming Thai place for my family to meet Ronan for the first time. To manage the antici-pated shock, we decided it was a good idea for Ronan to cover his tattoos for the time being—until they had made peace with the ear-rings and ponytail. One step at a time.

Ronan was standing in front of the restaurant wearing a slim, black long-sleeved shirt. I could tell he was nervous from a distance. As we approached, I introduced him to my parents. At the dinner table, I served as the official facilitator, bringing up topics to mini-mize awkwardness, switching between languages, and cracking some jokes. My dad spoke perfect English, but my mum didn't understand everything, so I made sure she wasn't left out of the conversation.

When there was silence for more than five minutes, and I couldn't think of a relevant topic for discussion, I decided to share Ronan's story with my parents in Arabic. After I was done, I turned to Ronan and asked, '*Sah?*' (which means 'right?' in Arabic). Automatically he responded with a cute '*Sah!*'

My parents laughed out loud in surprise. This simple three-letter word in Arabic broke the ice. And the rest of the dinner flowed smoothly. My parents were lovely to him; they asked questions to genuinely get to know him. I knew my mother liked Ronan because she would have given him an attitude if she felt otherwise. I was so relieved.

A week after our successful dinner, I walked around the neighbour-hood with my parents. As Mum entered a fabric shop, I spotted a toy store that caught my attention. I scouted the store with hopes of finding something fun for Ronan. It was about five days before a Christmas party Ronan was hosting at his house. So I was on the lookout for a Christmas gift.

Behind the counter sat a large box adorned with a beautiful golden train. Instantly, a story Ronan had shared came rushing back to me. He didn't have much in his childhood, and his family led a modest life. When he was around eleven years old, his father told him that his uncle would be visiting from Paraguay for Christmas and bringing him a massive train that would zoom around a track, complete with sounds. His father had intended to bond with Ronan through this tale, never suspecting the impact it would have. However, young Ronan eagerly awaited his uncle's arrival every day for a month, stationed by the door. When Christmas passed, he finally realised that the train would never come.

Until I found it in the corner of that store, that is—I knew I had found the perfect Christmas gift. When I came out of the store with the huge box, I said, 'Guys, look what I got Ronan for Christmas!'

As I lifted the box to display it, I saw every cell contributing to my mother's facial expressions change drastically. 'Didn't you say that he was learning about Islam?'

That remark instantly triggered and offended me, causing me to roll my eyes in response. The notion that Ronan's potential conversion would imply he couldn't celebrate Christmas if he chose to seemed absurd to me. After all, I celebrated Christmas and numerous other holidays alongside my friends, regardless of my own religious affiliation. Appreciating and respecting someone else's religious traditions did not require me to adhere to their faith.

My parents refrained from bringing up Ronan for the remainder of their visit. My mother, convinced that Ronan's conversion was insincere, grew opposed to our marriage. She consistently voiced her disapproval to my father in an attempt to garner his support. However, my father remained impartial and distanced himself from the ensuing drama. Whenever I sought his perspective on the matter, he would express his trust in my judgment. After the turn of the year, my parents returned to Sudan, and for the following twelve months, they made no inquiries about Ronan's well-being. It was as if he had never existed. I understood that my mother's hope was for the subject to fade away by avoiding any mention of it, allowing her to relinquish her concerns.

While I pretended I didn't care about being given the silent treatment, I did. I felt hurt that they would dismiss something so important to me. And just as they didn't ask, I decided I wouldn't share anything related to my relationship with them. Despite my resolve, my mother's obvious disapproval slowly started to get to me subconsciously. I began to question the relationship with Ronan. I questioned if we were studying Islam hard enough. I questioned why he should even convert in the first place. I wondered whether our relationship was a sin. I asked if we even had a relationship.

My love for Ronan was immeasurable. He embodied the qualities I had always yearned for in a partner. His saintly nature was evident through his unwavering kindness, boundless compassion, genuine love, and honesty. Simply being in his presence uplifted and transformed me, making me strive to be a better version of myself. The mere thought of losing him shattered my heart into countless fragments.

Simultaneously, I grappled with the notion of Ronan converting to my faith. While I cherished my beliefs, I didn't want to impose them on him. I was willing to provide him with any information or guidance he sought, but I refused to exert any pressure or influence on his decision. Amidst the confusion that consumed me, one thing remained unequivocal: I would never manipulate Ronan into converting. That was a boundary I would steadfastly uphold.

In pursuit of that objective, I found myself acting unnaturally. I became cautious about my words, carefully avoiding any mention of Islam unless Ronan explicitly inquired. I restrained myself from sharing the remarkable aspects of my faith, even when I stumbled upon something worth discussing.

It was hard to wear a mask around the one I loved in a bid to protect him. Juggling between the pain of not having my family's support and tip-toeing around Ronan, I slowly gave up on the crazy idea of marrying someone different. When I couldn't handle it a moment longer, I broke down. I told Ronan what was going on inside my mind.

He paused pensively and asked me, 'Let me ask you this, babe, every time that I teach you about new health hacks, encourage you to go to the gym, and send you all the links about biohacking, do you think I am manipulating you to convert to my lifestyle out of ill will?'

'Of course not. You are just trying to teach me things that would make me healthier.'

'Then why do you think you are manipulating me if you share something about Islam that has impacted your life? It's exactly the same thing. It's just that when it comes to religion, we start to freak out and put all kinds of labels on it. I want you to share everything you love about it at any moment. And remember babe, I am the person who's making that decision at the end of the day.'

The relief to hear these words from Ronan was indescribable.

As my parents' return drew near, anxiety started to creep in. I found myself dreading the idea of Ronan meeting them, wanting to avoid going through the same struggles again. However, Ronan insisted that we had to face it. He believed that if we wanted to be together, we had to fight for our relationship.

He was right, but I dreaded that truth. The closer my parents' arrival date came, the more sleepless nights I had. I would lie in bed and imagine all the annoying things my mum would say, and every cell in my body would get triggered with anger. I tortured myself with all the possible worst-case scenarios, to the point of tears. I lived everything I didn't want to happen in my mind before they even arrived.

But seeing the giant smile on my parents' faces at the airport reminded me of the unconditional love that I often forgot. I instantly realised how much I had missed them, too. As long as we didn't talk about Ronan, love was all around us.

Meeting the Folks, Round Two

I prepared tea for our evening chill time. I dragged the coffee table closer to my mother and placed her cup next to the date cookies she had baked. She re-adjusted her body and reached out to take her first sips of the tea.

I sat beside her, battling to choose my first sentence. Fighting through the resistance, I shouted the first words with no warning.

'Ronan wants to come and see you guys.'

'Ronan? There's still a Ronan? Didn't we close this topic already?'

'Of course, there's Ronan. You think he will magically disappear because you stopped talking about him?' The bitterness in my words surprised even me.

'Olla, you know my take on this. We can't accept someone who is not a Muslim. This is our faith, and we can't play around with that. Your dad and I don't see him as a person who would take that step. And there's nowhere to go from here.'

'Mama, the only reason you are saying that is because you made up a story in your mind ever since you saw that gift for Christmas. You need to understand that what we are going through is a journey, and whether we celebrate Christmas or not is irrelevant to that journey. You can't jump to conclusions without knowing all sides of the story.'

My mum was visibly taken aback. But much to my dismay, she continued, 'It's not just that. As a person, Ronan is not a man I see for you. He seems boyish and doesn't look responsible enough to care for a family. He doesn't suit you.'

'And you have concluded that from one dinner? You don't know him, Mama. Everything you say is your speculation because you didn't even try to get to know him.'

'And how do you suggest I do that? Anyway, it's my intuition talking, and a mother's intuition is always on point.'

The conversation saddened me. I often portrayed a tough exterior to match my mum's, but those words made it tough to keep it up. Deep inside, I desperately wanted her approval and support. But at the moment, I failed to see how that would happen. That day I went to see Ronan to share this conversation I had my mum. My heart wanted to censor most of it, but we had promised to tell each other everything.

'I am sorry about what my mother said,' I apologized and hugged him.

'Don't be. This is all new and different for her. She is doing her best with what she knows, right?'

'I wish she was here to hear you say that. I wish she could see what an amazing human you are. Ronan, I can't see the light at the end of this tunnel anymore. I just can't.'

'Olla, if your parents are not on board, are you willing to do this without them?'

I couldn't speak. Ronan held my face and looked me in the eye. 'Are you thinking of giving up on us, babe?'

Tears ran down my face.

'I don't know.'

Ronan covered his face and started to shake as he cried out loud. I had never seen him cry before, and my heart broke when I did. I held him in my arms, and we both cried. I didn't even know how long we stayed in the position, but it felt like hours. When there were no more tears to cry, Ronan looked at me.

'At least we are crying because we want to be together, not the other way around.'

Surrender to Faith

After my parents left, I decided to stop trying to force things. It had been two years since I had introduced Ronan to my parents, and, mentally, I was exhausted.

I began to find quiet and solitude, intentionally simplifying my daily activities. I sought solace in prayer and meditation to find my grounding again. Within the stillness, I confronted the pain that resided within me. There was so much pain, and the quieter I got, the more I felt it. But I knew that the only way out was through.

So, I picked up my journal again.

Every morning, I would put pen to paper about the emotions I felt, the things that hurt me the most, everything I wished I'd said, my fears, and my loneliness. More often than not, I would stop halfway because my tears would interrupt the process.

My body felt these emotions, too; my neck and shoulders were tight, and I had gastric cramps and headaches. I was constantly grinding my teeth, and my jaw ached. I had more health issues during this period than I had had in my entire life. Those were alarming signs. Reducing these symptoms would be my guide to gaining my wellness again.

Every time I journaled, I would meditate and visualize the incidents that hurt me and try to forgive them. I needed to let go. I did that for months. With time, I started to feel some ease within myself.

Ten days before Ramadan, I was reading a book with my feet on the couch in the far corner of the office. Ronan came, dragged a chair, and sat beside me, beaming. 'Hello, there,' I said, smiling.

'Babe, I've decided to convert.'

I took a minute to let it sink in, and then I asked him why.

'I've done a lot of thinking and reflecting in the past few months, and the concepts I've learned about Islam don't sound too foreign. I understand and believe in these concepts. I am certain this is what I want to do in my heart. And I want to do it this weekend before Ramadan, so I go through my first fasting month as a Muslim.'

I had no words to say to him. All I was capable of doing was hugging him.

On Saturday, we took an Uber to the National Mosque in Kuala Lumpur. Completely clueless about how this process worked, Ronan told the guard at the entrance, 'I am here to convert. Where do I go?'

Astounded, the guard jumped out of his chair and said, 'I will take you, sir.'

The guard walked us to an office within the premises of the mosque. We were greeted by a Malaysian lady who gave us a warm smile when we entered. After explaining what we had come to do, the lady said, '*Mashallah, Mashallah*, please have a seat. Let me see if the Sheikh is still around.'

The Sheikh, a man in his seventies with a long white ponytail, grey eyes, and the smile of an angel, walked toward us. He shook our hands and asked Ronan to sit on a chair facing him. After he shared his background with us and asked us to do the same, he said, 'So, Ronan, you want to convert to Islam, is that correct?'

'Yes.'

'Are you being forced by anyone to convert to Islam?'

'No.'

'Are you converting to Islam by your free will?'

'Yes.'

'Very good. To convert to Islam, you must recite the *Shehada* after me, a declaration of your new faith. Do you have any concerns or questions about that?'

'No.'

The Sheikh asked Ronan to lift his right hand with his index finger pointed up and repeat after him. Ronan lifted his finger and repeated the *Shehada* word for word.

'Congratulations, my son.' The Sheikh gave Ronan a hug. We all took a picture together, and they brought some sweets and drinks to mark the occasion.

Ronan and I went through our first Ramadan together. I gave him a crash course on making the most out of the experience: the tips and tricks to keeping the body hydrated during fasting, the philosophy, the community aspect, the importance of giving back, and evening prayers—all the nuggets that make Ramadan so magical.

And indeed it was. Ronan and I had the most incredible experience together. He dived in with an open mind and an open heart. He loved it so much that he continued fasting even after Ramadan ended. Going through Ramadan together bonded us in ways we would never have expected.

From Rio

A couple of months later, we took a trip to Brazil to see Ronan's family. When he had told them that he'd converted to Islam, they were not best pleased, to say the least. This was understandable. Ronan's parents were raised as Christians and they raised him that way as well. His parents had always treated me like their own daughter whenever I visited them in Brazil. So, I was worried that after he told them about his conversion, they would start treating me differently. And that would suck because I had so much love and respect for them.

His parents rushed towards us when we walked out of the arrivals gate. They hugged Ronan in tears, and much to my surprise, they came to give me a hug, too. It was like none of the tension existed. Moments like these always remind me of the magnitude of the love parents have for their children.

That evening, Ronan's mum prepared a big spread for dinner, all of our favourite Brazilian dishes. Before everyone sat for dinner, my phone rang. It was my mother. I hesitated to pick up for a minute and then decided to answer.

'Hi, Mum.'

'*Ahleen*, how are you?'

'I am good. You?'

'*Alhamdulillah*, all is good. How's everything? Work, Malaysia?'

'I am actually in Brazil right now.'

'What are you doing there?'

'I came to visit Ronan's family.'

'Why would you go all the way to visit them? You have no connection to them whatsoever. And didn't we agree that you would forget about this whole thing if Ronan didn't convert?'

'First of all, I do have a connection to his family. Second, Ronan did convert months ago. But since you never bother to check in or see what's happening in our lives, you never knew. And even if he didn't convert, I would still visit them.'

My mum's tune changed immediately. It deepened and slowed down.

'When did he convert?'

'In March. We fasted Ramadan together.'

'Still, it is not a reason to go to Brazil for his family.'

'Mum, I've got to go now. Bye.'

'Bye.'

I tried to shake it off. Everyone gathered around the dinner table, ready to eat. You could see the thrill and the sparkle in the eyes of

Ronan's family just being with him. I loved seeing them sharing stories and laughing out loud—I couldn't understand most of it due to the language barrier, but it was impossible to not feel their joy. At the same time, I felt some uneasiness about my conversation with my mother. But I tried to keep a smile on my face throughout dinner.

As the desserts were making their way to the dining table, Ronan turned to me and whispered in my ear, 'What do you think about sharing our plan to get engaged with my parents? I don't know when I will see them again, and it would be nice to tell them face to face.'

I didn't tell Ronan about the call I had with my mother. I was dubious about his premature announcement, but I said, 'Sure,' anyway. He beamed. 'Guys, I have something to share with you.'

The entire family went silent in anticipation.

'Olla and I have decided to get engaged at the end of this year, and we wanted to share this news with you!'

Ronan's family erupted in joy upon hearing the news. His sister embraced me tightly, tears of happiness welling in her eyes, followed by his parents. Each hug felt like a divine balm, easing the unease I had carried since the phone call. It was the support and encouragement I dearly craved at that instant. I felt loved and celebrated.

Lying in bed that night, I found myself lost in thoughts. The phone call with my mother had left feeling numb. It stirred up memories of the 'never good enough' standards I faced as a teenager. But in that quiet moment, I made a firm decision. It was time to embrace my adulthood and shed the desperate need for parental approval. I resolved to break free from their beliefs and fears, while still maintaining respect for them. I was ready to forge my own path and make life decisions on my own terms.

Choosing Love Over Fear

A few months later, as we waited for our sushi rolls to glide toward us on the conveyor belt, I turned to Ronan and felt the urge to share an idea with him.

'What is it, babe?' Ronan extended his hand to reach mine while looking straight into my eyes.

'I think we should do *Aqid* when my parents are here in December. *Aqid* is like one step higher than an engagement, and it's usually conducted by an Imam. It's like a marriage registration. If we do *Aqid*, we are officially married in the eyes of Islam. People usually do an engagement, the *Aqid*, then the wedding party. But I want us to skip to *Aqid* right away. I feel it will end the back and forth with my parents. I want this to be a closed case. It's been three years since you met them, and I'm done with the mental torture. What do you think?'

Ronan smiled and answered, 'I think it's a wonderful idea. I will marry you today if you let me!'

I knew I needed to inform my parents of our decision about *Aqid*. But I wanted to start with my siblings first. I relished their support and their tips. And just as I imagined, they were all in.

Alyaa: '*Ya Salam*, this is the best news ever. It's about time, Sis! I love Ronan, and I know he will be an incredible husband. It's great that you're telling Mum a couple of months before it happens, so if she has any steam to release, you will be far away. Ha ha!'

Assgad: '*Mabrouk*, Olla. So happy to hear that. I will start planning to come with the kids to celebrate with you. Tell Mama, and I will call her after to manage any emotions.'

Attaf: '*Alf Mabrouk wallai*. I am so happy for you and can't wait to meet Ronan. I've heard fantastic things about him and am excited for both of you.'

Abbas: '*Alf Mabrouk, Aloyia*. You are finally joining the club. And don't worry about Mum. After my experience marrying my Turkish wife, I know how to manage Mama's emotions. I got your back.'

Once I had my dose of the Abbas family consultation, I dialled my mum's number. 'Aloo?'

'Hi Mama, how are you?'

'*Alhamdulillah*. How are you?'

'You sound so happy; what's going on?' I asked sarcastically.

'I am. Attaf decided to have his *Aqid* next week.'

'Yes, he told me. I am so happy for him.'

As my mother continued to discuss her plans for the *Aqid*, I wondered if she would be equally as happy for me. After about half an hour of conversation, I felt it was the right moment to share my own plans with her. Without overthinking, I casually inserted my words, 'Speaking of *Aqid*, Mum, I'm planning to have mine in December when all of you visit.'

Silence occupied the space for a few seconds. Those seconds felt like an hour for me. I felt my body getting warm and my face starting to sweat. Finally, she replied.

'Darling, if that's what you want, and in your heart you know that Ronan's intention is pure and sincere towards God and towards you, I have no issues with it whatsoever. As your parents, we release ourselves from that responsibility and hand it over to you.'

Although I could feel that my mum was not head over heels for the news, I was still relieved by her response. Her acceptance made me notice something: all this time, I had been upset about Mum's expectations about my future spouse, while I had my own expectations about how she should behave toward my choice!

I made a conscious effort to let go of my defensiveness and view things from my mother's perspective. I realised that this was a new experience for her, and she was doing the best she could with the knowledge she had. Her actions came from a place of love and protection for me.

By recognising and accepting her intentions, a significant burden of resentment that I had been carrying was lifted from my shoulders. I felt a sense of release and freedom, as I no longer held onto negative emotions towards my mother.

A few months later, it was time for my parents to come for their end-of-the-year holiday. This time, my sisters were flying in as well. On a Friday night, Dad, Mum, Assgad, Alyaa, Ronan, a few friends, and I gathered at my house for the *Aqid* ceremony. I wanted to keep it simple and have only those closest to us attend.

The beautifully decorated living room had flowers, candles, music, and a delightful spread of desserts and drinks. Ronan, accompanied by his best friend, arrived looking sharp, bearing thoughtful gifts and flower bouquets. Following tradition, the groom's entrance preceded mine as the bride-to-be. I walked out of hiding into the living room to the sounds of my Arab friends making *Zaghrouta* (high-pitched vocal sounds representing trills of joy) as I went to give Ronan a hug.

A professor from the Islamic University, sent by the Sudanese Embassy, arrived to officiate the *Aqid*. Sitting in the middle between my father and Ronan, he asked them to hold hands and repeat after him. Then he turned to look at me to ask if I approved of this marriage.

'I do,' I said.

And in a few minutes, we were married.

The happiness on my parents' faces dissolved all the years we had struggled leading up to this moment. I had craved that sentiment so badly, and I indulged it fully. We laughed, danced, ate, and took hundreds of pictures. It was beautiful.

As people bid farewell, I returned to my room and approached the closet. Opening the drawer that housed my essential items, I retrieved the passport I had needed for the *Aqid* and prepared to return it to its rightful place. However, as I pulled open the drawer, a familiar sight caught my eye—my little blue notebook with its lock. It slipped from the drawer, but I swiftly saw it before it hit the ground, feeling a rush of nostalgia as it rested in my hands. A smile adorned my face as I succumbed to the irresistible temptation to unlock and scan its pages, absorbing fragments of my thoughts and sentiments, until my fingers came to a halt on a page titled 'Love List.'

I was taken aback as I realised I wrote this page after my first heartbreak, and it had been penned approximately four years ago. My hand instinctively covered my mouth in surprise as I faced a forgotten relic of the past. Unable to resist the pull of curiosity, I settled onto the floor and eagerly delved into the words I had inscribed all those years ago.

> The man I am with is kind, loving, caring.
> He is motivating, passionate, and very supportive.
> He likes me precisely the way I am and knows all my flaws.
> He tells me I am beautiful every day.
> He is fit and healthy but doesn't mind enjoying life from time
>   to time.
> He cares about my feelings.
> He loves to travel and always plans surprise trips for us.

We enjoy fasting and praying, and we stay connected to our
    faith.

He is financially independent and ready to commit and have a
    beautiful family.

He loves me with all his heart and fights for our love.

He only makes me cry happy tears.

He is humble, generous, and loves to help people.

He is into personal growth.

He is kind and loving to my family, and his family is kind and
    caring.

My disbelief grew as I realised that the traits and qualities on the list
perfectly aligned with who Ronan was. In hindsight, it became appar-
ent that Ronan's entry into my life was not a mere coincidence. It was
as if God had orchestrated his arrival with meticulous intention.

Embarking on this journey with Ronan has been instrumental in
my personal growth. Through our multicultural marriage, I have
gained invaluable insights and wisdom. I have realised that despite
our diverse backgrounds, Ronan, this extraordinary person from a
distant land, is not so different from me. When love became our primary language, cultural barriers, customs, skin colours, and beliefs
faded into insignificance.

Moreover, I have come to understand that everything my parents did
was rooted in love. They were raised in a society that adhered strictly
to certain norms and perceived differences as wrongdoing, which
in turn bred fear of the consequences. Their actions were driven by
their desire to protect me. I have learned that sometimes we need

to walk our parents through the fear, enabling them to witness that what is on the other side isn't so scary.

This multicultural union also taught me to see the similarities we have as people instead of the differences. It taught me to fall deeper in love with my religion. But most of all, it taught me to choose love instead of fear!

After the *Aqid*, my parents took Ronan into our family as though he were one of their own. Once they moved from fear to love, they truly embraced Ronan, despite him coming from a place as far away from Riyadh as Rio.

From San Diego

CHAPTER 8

FROM SAN DIEGO

'Owning my story'

It had been six years since I'd joined Mindvalley, and what a ride it had been. With each passing year, my career soared to new heights, and my life transformed in ways I never thought possible.

I was traveling to numerous far-flung countries, exploring the stunning locations to plan some of the most unique experiences. I stayed at luxurious destinations where I would be cared for from arriving until leaving. I never had to worry about travel expenses, which made the experience of exploring multiple countries on different continents feasible. Despite traveling frequently, I never lost sight of the incredible privilege it was to experience new countries and cultures. I tried my level best to always remind myself not to take this freedom for granted.

I also loved that I was constantly learning from the best and was surrounded by inspiring people. But the most rewarding part was witnessing the impact of what I was doing firsthand. People who attended the events we organized came with lots of hopes and dreams. For some, it was about finding an answer to a question that had kept them stuck. For others, it was about finding inspiration for their next chapter in life. Some came to find love.

My job was far more than organizing an event. It was about designing a space where everyone would feel embraced and seen, a space where everyone felt comfortable being who they are. The goal was to make everyone feel at home. Understandably, I was very passionate about that. During events, I would observe people's journeys unfold. With time, it was easy to see that the number one reason people kept returning was to have a place where they felt they belonged.

That was when all the hard work in designing such experiences was justified. The inspiring stories of the people I met during these events have always been the cherry on top. Creating a space that felt like 'home' for others kept the fire and passion for what I did alive.

I Said 'Yes'!

One evening, as I multitasked between making dinner and grooving to my favourite 90s R&B music, a voice message from my CEO, Vishen, popped up on WhatsApp.

'Hey, Olla, I have this idea of having the team introduce themselves throughout the next Mindvalley events, and since you are leading the upcoming one, are you open to doing an opening speech? You can choose what you want to talk about. Okay, let me know.'

I paused Usher's music and replayed the message again. 'Speak in front of a thousand people? Me?'

Ordinarily, my immediate response to such a request would be a rational, 'No. Thanks.' But this was no ordinary day. It was an extraordinary opportunity to take the Mindvalley stage, one of the most powerful platforms. Moreover, the fact that Vishen himself proposed the idea demonstrated his unwavering confidence in my abilities.

One of the many qualities I admired in Vishen, both as a leader and person, was his genuine commitment to nurturing the growth of those around him. He consistently believed in my potential and motivated me to reach greater heights. Vishen's support and guidance opened countless doors for Ronan and me on our personal and professional development journey. I held his trust in high regard and reciprocated by placing my trust in his guidance.

So, I silenced my doubts and sent a voice message saying, 'That sounds great. Count me in.'

I put down my phone and felt my insides churn.

We were about two weeks away from our biggest event at that time. I was swamped with all the last-minute preparations. And being a perfectionist, every detail mattered. We had people flying from all over the world, hoping to go through a transformational experience. It was a big responsibility, one I never took lightly. So adding a speech to my never-ending to-do list was something I knew would be challenging.

I needed to figure out what I would talk about—and how to gather the courage to do it. But I knew I would get there.

Three days before I made my way to San Diego, where the event was going to be held, I still didn't have a speech ready. Amid the mental and physical chaos surrounding me, I closed my laptop and headed to my little meditation corner in my house. I had a big white carpet there, with cushions, essential oil diffusers, crystals, and plants. It was my go-to spot whenever I felt stressed. I closed my eyes and asked myself,

'If I were to open up my heart fully, what would it say?'

'How can I be genuine in my message, so that everyone hearing it feels connected to me?'

'Why was I selected to do this speech? Why me?'

I focused on my breathing and took deep and full breaths. I allowed my mind and my body to get calmer and calmer. And then the following thoughts came loud and clear;

'For this speech, I want to be raw. I want to be honest. I want to share a piece of me that I have kept hidden. I want to share my story.'

My Mess, My Message

It was 6 am in San Diego. I prayed Fajr and remained on my mat with my eyes closed. I visualized that I was on the stage, looking out at the crowd and connecting with every single person. I pictured a white beam of light going from my heart to theirs.

I then visualized that I was engulfed by the energy of support from the audience. I saw myself standing straight, confident, and comfortable. I pictured myself feeling excited to be on stage. I had a big smile on. I was walking across the stage with authority and ease. I saw myself concluding my speech and bowing my head slightly in gratitude for the applause that filled every corner of the room. My body tingled with so much gratitude for the vision. I opened my eyes and took a deep breath.

'I can do this.'

I remember repeating this sentence to myself every time my heart skipped a beat at the thought of speaking on stage. On top of my speech, I still had to run the entire event and ensure everything was going according to plan. It was intense, to say the least.

It was time to open the ballroom doors. The music was pumping. My Zumba dancers were ready at the centre of the stage for the opening. The team was behind the doors on standby, waiting for my signal.

'Here we go, guys; let's open doors!' I commanded and watched as an endless stream of people came in, full of energy and excitement. They moved in perfect synchronicity to pursue their seats. I signalled for the music to fade out so the host could take the stage. The host welcomed everyone in and introduced the CEO onto the stage. 'This is it. Here we go,' I sighed nervously.

I took the microphone and stood at the edge of the stage, ready to be called any second. The microphone was sliding smoothly through my palms. I rubbed them against my clothes in hopes of controlling the overproduction of sweat that was going on. Then I heard Vishen say, 'To open this event, I would like to welcome a special woman who put her heart into the preparation of this event and is here to share a few words with you. Please help me welcome Olla Abbas!'

I walked up the steps, hugged Vishen, and continued to the middle of the stage. I scanned the room for a second. With the reflection of the stage lights in my eyes, I could only see a sea of heads. I took a breath and lifted my microphone close to my mouth, ready to share a story I had never shared before the incident with the cleaner.

This was not a story I relished sharing in front of a thousand people I didn't know, but something in me insisted that I should. Sharing this secret I had held for so long would help me release it. In hindsight, I can see that it was a way to reprogram my belief of 'not being heard' as a teenager. After having a thousand pairs of ears listen to the story, I had no more excuse to hold on to it.

There was only one way to express such a personal story, with total transparency and vulnerability. Every word flowed directly from my heart, and they were generated effortlessly.

I had never been so present.

At one point, I became conscious of watching myself tell my story. I watched my body move back and forth across the stage. I watched the people listening and nodding, just like in a movie. It was a surreal experience.

'Thank you very much,' I completed my speech.

I bowed slightly and was ready to step off the stage. I then began to notice the crowd get up from their seats, one after the other. I froze in place, shocked at the standing ovation. My eyes teared up as I heard the applause of those celebrating a side of me that I had been ashamed of all my life. When I was preparing my humble speech, 'Your Stories Are the Lego Bricks of Your Life,' I didn't think for a second that it would get this kind of reaction. My intention was just to be raw and honest.

At the bottom of the stage, I was received by my teammates with hugs. Coming down those stairs, I knew something in me had shifted forever. But I didn't realize that this speech would also cause a shift in others. Hundreds of women thanked me for my courage to speak up about something so sensitive and challenging. I had no idea that some of these women were hearing their own stories being told from the stage.

Even after the event, I received messages from both men and women who had watched the speech on YouTube.

'I am inspired by how you shared your story from such an empowering stand, not a victimized one.'

'How did you heal from the pain of the incident?'

'My mother did the same thing. How did you forgive her?'

'Something similar happened to me. How did you find the courage to share such a story? I am still afraid to share mine.'

That's when I discovered something profound. Once I'd told my story, I didn't merely feel that a load had come off my shoulders; rather, all the negative emotions I had held towards the incident shifted into something positive and empowering. It was as if I was immersed in a pool of healing. The magnitude of love I felt in that room was indescribable. And I sensed it penetrating every cell of my soul.

For decades, I had walked around with a mask, trying to hide the shame and guilt of that incident. Burying this story in my mind caused effects that had limited my growth. But when I was ready to share it, I was given the platform to do so. Saying the story out loud made me see it through a different lens. It was no longer the lens of shame, victimhood, anger, or weakness. It made me see my story as my strength!

When I owned my story, I moved from pain to power.

I was asked to do the same speech for another event a couple of months later. And I did.

The following year, I gathered the courage to request stage time to do another speech in front of thousands of people. Once again, I chose to share a story from the heart. This time my speech was 'What It's Like to Be a Black, African, Muslim Woman.'

And the year after, I did; 'What is Home?'

I thought it would be easier after a couple of speeches. But it wasn't. Sharing a piece of my life with this level of truth and vulnerability was never comfortable. And every single time, I would go through the same emotional rollercoaster of fear, doubt, stress, and anxiety. But the liberty, power, and healing I felt after every speech helped me resist the shackles of my comfort zone.

As I stepped off the stage from one of my speeches, I was approached by Rajesh Setty, a successful entrepreneur, business advisor, and author of sixteen books (thus far), with his first book published at the age of thirteen. Rajesh hugged me and proclaimed, 'Olla, I have listened to a couple of your talks, and I think you should write a book.'

From Zutphen

CHAPTER 9

FROM ZUTPHEN

'Psychological healing'

Life was good. I was living in my dream apartment in the heart of the city. I was excelling at work and doing things that kept me motivated, passionate, and fulfilled. I felt that I was personally and professionally growing while travelling the world and having remarkable experiences.

I had a beautiful relationship with a wonderful husband. I was surrounded by amazing people who made me feel special and loved. My family continued to be a source of support and happiness. So life was beyond good, except for one major part of it …

… me.

While I had everything I had ever wished for, my inner world was going through turmoil. I was struggling to feel connected and peaceful within. I would wake up every morning feeling uneasiness and heaviness in my heart. A million thoughts would race, as if they were competing in the Olympics. And right away, anxiety would start to build. Before I had gotten the chance to brush my teeth, I would have over-occupied my mental space by overplanning the day ahead and worrying about the time I didn't have to do it all.

I found myself lost in my thoughts, unaware of my surroundings. When I walked on the street, I didn't see the sky, hear the birds chirping, or even know what was happening around me. My mind was out of control, and I was trapped inside it.

With my mind so out of balance, so became other aspects of my daily life. I was often angry, annoyed, and unhappy. My mind chatter was so constant that sleepless nights became the norm, and sadness was a frequent visitor. I started to have panic attacks. And the worst part was that I didn't know the root cause.

I kept asking myself, 'Why do I feel this way?' To find myself in this state after all the healing I had been through was frustrating. After months of this, I needed to find a way out. Nothing I had done before seemed to help. I needed something different, something more profound. Something that would enable me to take control from my mind and place it in my heart again.

I needed psychological healing.

A Mind Trip

It was still dark outside. Ronan and I had to get ready to catch the 7 am train; actually, we had to take two trains from Amsterdam to reach the small town of Zutphen in the Netherlands. And for the very first time, I wished a commute to be way longer than it was. The trip to Zutphen was different from our holiday trips to discover Europe. Our quest for that day was much deeper than that.

During the one-hour commute, I watched how my mind used all its tricks to get me to turn around and head back to the hotel, and it had some convincing strategies. Mostly, it made me scared of what I was about to do. But if I have learned anything over the years, it is that when fear creeps up, I feel the fear and go ahead anyway. In this case, it was going ahead with my first ayahuasca ceremony!

An ayahuasca ceremony is part of the culture of some Amazonian tribes. A plant-based brew is prepared as a spiritual medicine for an individual to go through a cleansing and healing experience. Ayahuasca has become popular around the world among those seeking a way to open their minds, heal from past traumas, or simply experience a wild psychedelic journey.

I have always been very cautious when undergoing such procedures without a compelling reason. I persistently had strong reservations, especially in situations where the practice is illegal or carried out by non-professionals. In fact, I strongly discourage engaging in such practices at illegal centres without professional guidance.

After thorough research, I discovered a sense of reassurance in the fact that the healing centre in the Netherlands was government-approved and fully legalized. Additionally, the person responsible for conducting and overseeing the process was a certified professional psychologist who worked closely with the government to ensure the utmost safety and efficacy of the procedure throughout the country. This practice's potential for healing and transformation compelled me to consider it further.

With this level of professional supervision and support, I mustered the courage to take a leap of faith. Despite my lingering apprehensions, I was about to embark on this new and unfamiliar experience, ready to embrace the unknown.

Faster than I wanted, we arrived at Zutphen station, where the ceremony guide, Eva, waited for us with her dog. Eva was a lovely Dutch lady in her fifties with short hair infused with beautiful silver strands; she had the most welcoming energy.

She greeted us and drove us to the centre. Ayahuasca was legal in the Netherlands at that time, so it wasn't some dodgy destination she was taking us to, but a cute and cosy building surrounded by fields and woods outside a small town. One of my only conditions for this ceremony was that my session would be private for Ronan and me. So we had the centre all to ourselves, making the experience more comfortable.

We sat at a wooden dining table facing a terrace with a beautiful view of a green field. 'Nervous?' Eva looked at me and asked.

'I am very nervous,' I responded.

Ronan had done this ceremony in this centre before, so he was more comfortable and relaxed than I was.

'Don't worry, it will be a beautiful experience. The most important thing you need to remember is to let go. Go with the flow. If you try to control it, you might struggle with it. But it will be much easier if you trust and allow yourself to be guided. Another tip I have for you is to remind yourself that the journey will end soon, and you will eventually be out of it.' Eva said with a warm voice.

'Letting go of control. That's easy for me,' I joked.

'Letting go' was one of the things that worried me the most, and it was a major reason for my wanting to do this ceremony. Admittedly, I was a little bit of a control freak. As an event organizer, I planned everything and was obsessed with ensuring every situation was under control. I struggled to 'go with the flow.' So the idea of not having control over my mind was terrifying.

Eva asked us to change into something more comfortable and led us to a bigger room. Floor cushions, candles, and crystals designed a circle in the middle of the room, along with two beds on opposite sides. Beside each mattress was a glass of water, a sleep mask, and an empty bucket. The smell of incense and slow background music calmed the room's energy. We sat around the circle, and Eva asked us to share our intention for this ceremony. I was asked to go first.

'I intend to have ease in my mind. I want to cleanse and let go of past traumas, resentment, guilt, shame, negative or suppressed emotions toward anyone or anything. To forgive everyone who ever hurt me consciously or unconsciously, including forgiving myself. To allow space for more love to flow through my body, mind, heart and soul. To love, accept, and appreciate every cell in my body the way it is. To feel happy, grateful, and content.'

As all those words flowed out of me effortlessly, so did my tears. I looked at Ronan, and tears were streaming across his face. By the end of our intention setting, even Eva was crying.

It was time to take the ayahuasca. I hugged Ronan, and we both went to our beds on opposite sides of the room. We needed to stay apart to avoid interrupting each other's experiences. I took a deep breath, sipped the drink, covered my eyes with the sleep mask, and lay on the mattress, waiting for my journey to begin.

The first twenty minutes passed, and I felt nothing. I started to wonder if it was because I took a smaller portion than Ronan. As that thought ended, an overwhelming tingling sensation overtook my face. It was like my skin was growing bubbles. The tingling started to go to my neck and continued to travel down my chest, stomach, lower belly, legs, and finally, my feet.

My heart was pumping faster than the speed of light. Geometric shapes of all colours and sizes rushed out of control through my mind. I began to feel like I had lost control of all my senses. My breathing was getting heavier, and my heart continued pumping faster and louder. 'It's okay, it's okay. This is what was meant to happen. You knew this was meant to happen,' I said to myself in panic.

The colours and shapes got crazier. The background music started to feel louder and louder. And with every beat, I felt my body scattered across the room. When I couldn't handle it any longer, I removed my mask and opened my eyes. Everything stopped.

I gasped for air and placed my hand on my chest, feeling the rise and fall of my body. Eva saw me and rushed over. She sat right beside me and held my hand.

'Is it too much for you?' She asked with a gentle voice.

'Yes. Do I have to do this?'

'Darling, I have nothing to undo it. You have to go through it. Remember, just trust and go with the flow. If you fight it, you will struggle more. Trust it, and it will be over soon.'

I took a deep breath and recited: 'I can do this. I can do this. It will be over soon. I can do this.'

I pulled down my mask to cover my eyes. Instantly, my body was shattered all over the room with the beat of the music again. While the vivid colours and shapes dominated my vision, I kept one hand on my chest to feel my breath. That helped me remember that I was still there. I was also glad that I could talk to myself throughout the entire experience. So I repeatedly reassured myself, 'I am still here. I am okay. This will be over soon. I can handle this.'

After some time, the crazy shapes and colours began to subside, and my mind and body gradually started to freak out a little less. Slowly, my mind felt more serene and smooth. Once the crazy shapes and colours stopped occupying my mental space, I began to see images of things related to my life. They felt like messages.

I will always remember my first message. It was loud, clear, and spot-on: 'You need more self-love. You need to stop your body-shaming and replace it with an appreciation for how far your body has taken you in life.'

At that point in my life, I didn't realize how harsh I was towards my body. I had forgotten about my complicated relationship with it. In my mind's eye, I saw hundreds of black spots all over my body. 'This is where you have been storing all the shame and guilt,' my mind announced. I then saw the black spots extracted from my body, floating above me and disappearing.

Next, people from my life started to line up in front of me—family, friends, acquaintances, and even people I disliked, all queued up. I knew right away that this had something to do with forgiveness.

First up was my mother. I sobbed at the sight of her face. 'Mum, I have taken for granted all the sacrifices you've made in your life so I can have the life I'm living now. You gave up on your dreams and passions and, without resentment, dedicated your life to my siblings and me. And no matter how much you have given me, I demanded more! You are a human who was given the difficult task of figuring out the life of five other human beings with no instruction manual or proper guidance. How could you have possibly taught me something you didn't know? You were doing your best with the knowledge you had. You were not supposed to have all the answers, anyway. You are not God. Today, I know you have come to me for forgiveness, and I completely forgive you and ask for your forgiveness in return for all my shortcomings.'

The back of my head started to feel the dampness of the pillow soaked in my tears.

Then my father appeared. I forgave him for his shortcomings and asked him to forgive mine. My siblings, friends, and co-workers followed. And, finally, the cleaner who tried to molest me. I didn't know his name, and his features started fading away. But when he appeared in my mind, I felt my stomach turn. I cried some more before I could speak to him.

'I forgive you and wish you well in your life. I let go of the anger I had towards you.' That was all I could say.

In my mind, a giant ball of love moved towards my abdominal area as if clearing all the pain and resentment I had carried for years. The ball then travelled from my abdomen to where all the individuals stood in line and covered them until they disappeared from my vision. I felt my body starting to elevate from the mattress. I gripped its sides tightly to prevent my body from floating away. Feeling the bed reminded me that it was just in my head.

Insights continued to pour over me during the six hours of the ceremony. I received messages about work, relationships, plans, family, and issues I faced. I took mental notes of everything that came to me and trusted that I would remember it all after the ceremony. Although I still had no control over what was going on in my mind, I was more relaxed about it. Nonetheless, I kept wishing for it to be over. At some point, I felt a weird sensation in my abdominal area, and I couldn't tell if I needed to go to the bathroom. For a minute, I wondered if I could still perform human activities. I removed the sleep mask and opened my eyes. I took a deep breath in gratitude for being able to take a break from it all.

I positioned my hands against the mattress to try and get up. I felt like I was one hundred years old. Eva rushed to help. The trip to the bathroom took way longer than it usually does. Eva helped me back to the room and, finally, to the bed.

'How many hours has it been?' I had no sense of time.

'It's been five hours. You're almost there. You are doing such a great job.'

I felt a sense of relief knowing that the most challenging part had passed. I took a sip of water and closed my eyes again, hoping no more crazy shapes would appear. They didn't. The music no longer flung me from one side to another. It was more of a gentle sway.

Shortly after, Eva approached my bed and said: 'Are you ready to close the ceremony?' I nodded. 'Okay, we will close the ceremony in fifteen minutes. I will come and help you when it's time.'

For fifteen minutes, I lay down with no thoughts. It was the most peaceful I have ever felt.

The three of us gathered around the circle to close the ceremony. I felt weak, and everything around me was moving slower. We held hands and closed our eyes as Eva said, 'Thank you for this moment of coming back to this circle. For all the healing and cleansing that our bodies and minds went through. For the strength to go through this.'

I interrupted her. 'I'm so sorry, but I need my bucket.' Eva handed me the bucket, and I stuck my face into it to throw up the water I had drunk.

'I'm so sorry. Please continue.'

'Don't be sorry. That's part of the healing process.' Eva remarked with a smile and continued.

'Thank you for the strength you have given us to go through this experience. To clear the path from the past and open the way to the new. We sit here in infinite gratitude. And with this, we close our experience for today.'

We hugged each other and went to a table decorated with roses and candles. It was covered with delicious-looking food that Eva had prepared to break our fast—different types of bread, cheese, jam, and fruits. We ate and sat around the table, sharing our experiences. I didn't say much. I was indulging in the peace and serenity I felt. My mind was silent. No stories on the loop. No blame. No planning. Just presence. It was like I'd been born again.

A New Birth

I woke up the following day after sixteen hours of sleep. When I opened my eyes, I took a second to wonder if it was all a dream.

Walking outside that afternoon was like nothing I had experienced in my life. I felt weightless in every sense of the word. Even my surroundings felt lighter. Everything was moving at a slow pace. The trees swayed gently, the breeze was delicate, and the sun was soft. I knew the environment hadn't changed overnight, but my mind had. It was moving unhurriedly. No thoughts crashing into each other, no stress, no planning. My body felt relaxed as well. I indulged in this quietness and wanted to savour every moment. Flashes of the images and messages I had experienced during the ceremony popped up frequently, and I felt the urge to write down everything I remembered.

I started to document my thoughts in a small notebook I had brought with me. I was surprised by how much I remembered. With every image and message I wrote down, a stream of insights poured upon me. I kept writing for two hours, nonstop. When I finished, I had all the answers to why I had struggled before the ceremony.

For the past six years, I have spread myself thin between goals, projects, travel, and commitments. My overtime and annual leave kept being carried from one year to the next. And when I wasn't working, I had many things to do. I was always busy with house chores, exercising, seeing friends, or learning something new.

The list was always long. On those days I chose to take some time off to watch TV, I would feel guilty for not striking an item off my list. In other words, in my dictionary, 'resting' was defined as 'wasting time.'

Downloading all of those thoughts into my journal that morning, it hit me: all these years, I had suffered from Busyholism—the addiction to being busy. I was constantly on the run. Racing with nonstop intensity, my engines were burned out. As a result, I felt unbalanced, unhealthy, and unhappy.

In my journal, I asked myself, 'Why do I want to be busy all the time?' and 'What has busyness been doing for me that I wanted in my life?' I recognised that keeping busy was a way to escape and feel no emotion. I had been running away from … me. Losing control over my mind during the ayahuasca ceremony gave me no choice but to face that. No wonder self-love and forgiveness were the first things that popped up for me during the ceremony.

It was time to face myself and stop running away!

Befriending Emotions

Facing my emotions would require time to sit down, listen, and comprehend all the feelings I had put on the back burner. My first step to treating my 'busyness' addiction was simply to slow down. I decided to reduce both professional and personal goals for the year. I marked my working hours in the calendar and planned to finish work at a particular time every day. I sucked at work boundaries, but I had to learn to draw the line. The new goal was 'less is more.'

To be able to transition, I arranged to take a week off work. On the first couple of days into 'me time,' I unconsciously made a daily schedule to keep myself busy. When I woke up, I prayed, did yoga, and meditated. Then I cleaned and organized things around the house. I went for a walk and got some groceries in the afternoons. I would cook, watch TV, and then go for a workout. I also started an online psychology course. I had convinced myself I needed to apprehend my emotions better. I was reading two books at the same time as well. By the end of day one, I was as busy as I would have been working my full-time job!

In the following days, I reduced my activities by half. The fewer things I did, the harder it was for me to sit still. I was instantly bored and craved any entertainment to save me: food, TV, and even house chores were welcomed. Anything but silence.

On my fourth day, I came across this quote by Joe Dispenza: 'Thoughts are the language of the mind, and feelings are the language of the body.'

I contemplated that for a few minutes, and a light bulb lit up. 'Those feelings I keep running from are the only language my body can use to communicate with me.' I then realised that if I wanted to deal with my emotions, I had to understand what they were trying to communicate. To do that, I needed to listen. And to listen, I needed to pay close attention to my thoughts.

Since I struggled to sit still, I decided to write instead. I remember hunting around the house for a new notebook to dedicate to this.

There was one all blinged-up with rose gold that I had saved for a unique writing project; I opened the first page and started writing. As always, I kept it simple, writing my thoughts exactly as they came to me. I was on a roll. I couldn't stop writing. It felt good to take things from my head and put them into the notebook.

I arranged fixed times to write. Every day, when I woke up, I would take a glass of warm water with lemon, sit on the balcony, and write whatever came to me. The rule remained the same, no censoring or sugar-coating. I would write my thoughts exactly as they appeared in my head. No matter how weird or ugly.

The scheduled writing time helped me stay consistent. What felt strange was reading back the thoughts I had documented. It was scary to see the train of ideas that regularly went through my head. It made sense that my mind had done everything it could to distract me from sitting with my thoughts.

The more quiet time I had, the more I witnessed my thought patterns heading towards negative emotions. The guilt of not doing things perfectly. Unworthiness to be loved the way I was. Not liking my body. Fear of the future.

Having these written before me gave me no place to escape.

I noticed how having these thoughts going on a loop impacted me emotionally. I would feel deep sadness. Even when everything around me was better than good, how I felt inside wasn't. So I continued writing the thoughts that triggered these emotions.

With my mind not wanting to face it all, it was not easy to do this every day. Whenever negative emotions began to surface, I would fight the temptation to escape by watching a useless reality show with a large bowl of salted caramel ice cream. Truth be told, I did lose some of these battles. But, I would still journal my thoughts and feelings the following day. And throughout this process, I reminded myself of something I heard Michael Beckwith once say: 'Treat sadness as a companion, not the enemy.' That helped me resist fighting these types of emotions. Instead, I asked what they were trying to tell me.

Analysing my thoughts also revealed the number of limiting beliefs I'd hoarded over the years. The longer I kept them alive, the truer they became for me. My thought patterns circled around these beliefs:

I am not good enough.

I don't have what it takes to lead.

I am fat.

I am not safe.

I can't express myself.

I am not worthy.

And I knew this was only the tip of the iceberg. Just like an onion, there were so many layers I needed to peel off before I was able to get to the root of my beliefs—why I had them, how I got them, and most importantly, how I could reprogram them.

That's when I decided I needed help.

But asking for professional help was a challenging task. I hadn't grown up in a culture that praised asking for or accepting help. I needed to figure out how and where to start. The idea of displaying my life in front of a stranger was also challenging, but my gut told me that was what I needed to do.

Three days later, during a catch-up lunch, a friend of mine mentioned working with an Emotion Therapy coach who'd helped her during a tough emotional time. I asked her to connect me with the coach, and for the next six months, I had a therapy session once a week.

During my first sessions, I struggled to put my guard down. I stayed at a surface level every time I spoke about my emotions. But Jackie, my coach, called me out whenever I tried to tiptoe around my feelings. Eventually, I began to go a little deeper with every session.

Getting someone to guide me in handling my emotions was life-changing. In a matter of months, we worked on many deep-rooted beliefs and feelings that I hadn't been able to face for years. Every session revealed a side of me I didn't even know existed. It was the place where I could drop my mask and get absolutely raw and transparent. I believe that reaching this state was possible because I had been working on myself for years. I was peeling one layer at a time.

Different tools and practices have varying effectiveness during specific phases of our lives, and what worked for me may not be suitable for someone else at a different stage of their healing journey. While the Ayahuasca ceremony played a role in my healing, I personally do not feel compelled to revisit it, nor would I recommend it to others, especially if it is illegal and carried by non-professionals. The outcome and impact of such an experience can vary significantly from person to person. It is crucial to stay attuned to the needs of our body, mind, and soul and not simply follow trends or engage in activities solely because they are popular.

Each individual's path is unique, and it is vital to honour and listen to ourselves when determining what truly resonates with us. In my healing journey, I found therapy to be an invaluable tool that provided the support and guidance I needed during that particular stage. Therapy offered a personalized approach that addressed my specific needs and helped me navigate my healing process in a meaningful and beneficial way.

Prioritizing, dedicating, and investing time and effort into delving into my mind proved crucial. It illuminated the extraordinary influence of the mind on every other aspect of my life. I grasped the significance of cultivating tranquility and embracing acceptance within my mind, recognising its pivotal role in harmonizing essential facets of my existence—body, heart, and soul. I realised that residing on obsessive, negative, and fearful thoughts created a turbulent inner landscape, rendering daily functioning nearly impossible. Yearning for equilibrium, I desired to cultivate an inner sanctuary within my mind to navigate the world with clarity and purpose.

After eight months of confronting my emotions and beliefs, I started feeling myself again. My sessions also helped me tap into one of my most complicated relationships, the one with my body.

An Intervention with My Body

I have had a love-hate relationship with my body for as long as I can remember.

In Riyadh, I was close to two of my cousins, Wijdan and Shahad. We were about the same age, and we did everything together. At that time, Riyadh didn't have any entertainment. Cinemas, concerts, festivals—none of that was available. Besides parks, the only amusement we had was shopping and food.

To cater to the high demand, Riyadh had incredibly delicious food everywhere. We would eat out, go shopping, or watch movies on weekends while snacking on junk food. My cousins had these tall, naturally slim bodies that seemed to erase any traces of junk food as soon as it was consumed. I, on the other hand, was gaining weight skilfully. I dreaded every extra kilo. But it was tough to control my diet when it was the primary source of entertainment where I lived.

As soon as the fun was over, I struggled to look at my reflection in the mirror. I didn't like how chubby my hips and butt looked. Keeping up with the 90s fashion of super-low-waisted jeans and cropped tops was impossible. I desperately wanted the weight to come off, so throughout my teenage years, I went from one failed diet to another. Ultimately, I figured out that the only way I could enjoy my time with my cousins without gaining weight was to become bulimic.

I would go out, eat fast food, and snack all night. Once everyone was gone, I would feel guilty for the food I ate and go to the bathroom to throw it up. At some point, I became so good at it that I didn't even need to force my finger down my throat to empty my stomach. I just had to stand in front of the toilet bowl and think about it, and I would immediately feel nauseated. I would brush my teeth and go to bed as if nothing had happened. I practiced this routine for years, not knowing I had a 'condition.'

One day, when everyone had gone, I began my regular routine. But this time, the food got stuck halfway through. I choked and immediately started panicking. I felt my heartbeat rise fast. I bent over more, I tried to adjust my body quickly to different positions to help get rid of the food I felt in my throat. Thankfully, it came out.

I could have continued choking, and no one would have been able to help me. I could have died. That was my wake-up call. I stopped throwing up, but I continued hating my body.

After I graduated from university in Malaysia and joined Mindvalley, I found myself in an environment that made me slowly transition to healthier eating habits. There was no junk food lying around in the office. People were making green smoothies, cooking low-carb meals, and snacking on nuts and fruits. The team would choose healthier restaurants whenever we went for lunch. Being surrounded by health-conscious individuals intrinsically made me want to be healthier too. Slowly, my body improved, aided by some practices I had picked up, like yoga and movement classes.

Despite losing a lot of weight since I moved to Malaysia and making much progress with my lifestyle, I was still very judgmental of my body. I struggled to appreciate what I saw in the mirror, instead seeing the flaws and wishing I could change them. My best friends used to respond to some of my remarks about my body by saying, 'Babe, I think you see yourself much bigger than you actually are!'

When I heard that from multiple people, I wondered if my chubby teenage self existed only inside my mind.

It was a Friday night when my girlfriends and I decided to hit our favourite sushi joint in KL. We loved every item on the menu and frequently ordered all of them. Our table was so full of dishes that the staff had to drag another one over to fit everything. I hadn't realised how much I'd eaten until I had to stand up. I felt like I couldn't carry the weight of my stomach—but we were not done yet!

We ended the night with one of our favourite vegan ice creams. When I arrived home, I felt an overwhelming sensation from all the food sitting in my stomach. I went to the bathroom to clean my makeup, and out of nowhere, I found myself going toward the toilet bowl and preparing my mind to activate the process of throwing up. To my surprise, I could do it precisely the same way I did seven years ago.

When I lay in bed that night, I felt sad about what I had done. I couldn't enjoy indulging in food occasionally without the fear of gaining weight. Worse was the fear of finding myself in the same state I'd been in as a teenager. Operating from fear made me punish my body more than appreciate it. Because loving my body was one of the first messages I received in my ayahuasca ceremony, I brought the topic up during my therapy sessions. For four months, the only thing we spoke about was my body. The more we dug, the more we needed to go deeper and deeper.

All along, I believed that I only disliked my body because of how it looked. But my therapy revealed a whole other dimension. Shame.

There was so much shame towards my body that I had to uncover and heal. I realised that I had felt shame from that first incident, when I was molested by a stranger as a little girl. And I continued building on that shame, year after year. I was actually a very skinny child all through my childhood. A part of me now believes that the weight was my body's way to feel safe and keep away the predators. I always had this conflicting desire both to feel pretty, as any other girl would, *and* to be invisible when I was in new places with new faces.

Growing up in a culture that desired I hide my woman's body in every way possible didn't help either. But the biggest shame was my sexuality. I learned this right off the bat. Sexuality wasn't to be mentioned or discussed. It needed to be ignored and hidden at all times. Shame was everywhere, and it was only natural that my relationship with my body was built on that foundation.

As my therapy sessions continued to heal me mentally, I felt the urge to match that healing physically. So I decided to start taking care of my body as a form of practicing self-love. I didn't want to jump into a diet to shrink myself this time. Instead, I wanted to learn more about the food I was consuming and its effect on my body. I set a goal to work with my body, listen to what it was trying to communicate, and feed it what it needed.

There was no manual on how to go about my goal, so I trusted that my intuition would lead the way. As I read more about nutrition, I became aware of the problems with food sold in supermarkets. The more I learned about the food industry, the more I wanted to keep their products out of my kitchen. Whenever I went to the grocery store, I had less variety to choose from than before.

I moved a little more as well. I walked a little farther every day while swimming and doing yoga several times a week. I felt lighter, less bloated, and at ease with the process. I became less abusive with the food I was feeding my body and the words I was feeding my brain. My biggest motivation was how I felt. Every day, I felt a little stronger, lighter, and prettier.

Learning about food and nutrition allowed me to have better contact with my body, and two concepts helped rehabilitate my beliefs about it. First was the idea that my body is a unique and complex work of art that knows what works best for itself. Somebody else's idea of what my diet should be might not actually work for me. The key was to test different things and choose what felt good. And the second concept was to stop trying to make my body look like something it was not.

Every time I had tried a diet, I'd wanted to look like someone I saw on TV or in a magazine. A strategy set for failure. I had to learn that

I have a unique shape that might not resemble another person's, and I needed to love it because it existed. Changing the stories that were on 'replay' for years in my head about my body image wasn't easy. But I was on my way there.

The notion of shrinking my food to shrink my body, which is the typical dieting formula, wasn't for me anymore. I wanted to switch scarcity to abundance. I substituted the idea of *Removing* things from my diet to *Replacing*.

I replaced regular milk chocolate bars with 90% Cacao chocolate bars, and with time, I couldn't stand milk chocolate anymore because it was too sweet. I substituted sushi wraps for bread wraps. I also tried shiitake noodles for regular noodles and enjoyed them. I replaced sodas with kombucha. Whenever I felt like having pizza, I created a homemade cauliflower pizza, which was just as delicious. I also experimented with protein cakes and oat cookies for desserts. I found an alternative for almost any dish I enjoyed in the past. I didn't feel limited to just eating grass and meat. With time, I found myself transitioning to healthier choices. My energy was very high compared to how I used to feel. I was also having way fewer gastric pains and bowel issues.

After a couple of months, I wanted to move more. In my quest to become more active, I decided to join a gym. It was there that I discovered a newfound interest in weightlifting. Gradually, I started attending classes and eventually began training on my own. I learned to tune in to my body's cues and adjust my workouts accordingly. Some days, specific exercises didn't feel right, so I respected those signals. On other days, I opted for lighter weights. I made it a priority to listen to and honour my body's needs throughout my fitness journey.

The more I listened to what my body needed, the more enjoyable the experience was. I was at the gym three times a week without fail and craved it when I was travelling and couldn't go.

After a year of healthier habits and active living, what started as an 'experiement' transformed into a lifestyle. But this journey wasn't without its challenges. The harsh truth was that I had been numbing my body's cries for help with food, ignoring its pleas to heal. But I came to realize that healing my mind was the key to unlocking my body's full potential. With each step, I shed limiting beliefs and fears and embraced a new positive perspective. The transformation was nothing short of miraculous.

I look in the mirror and see a body that's not just a shell, but a masterpiece. A body that's strong, resilient, and capable of so much. It took me over twenty years to fall back in love with the only home I've had for every moment of my existence. And that was the most profound healing of all.

From
Sharjah

CHAPTER 10

FROM SHARJAH

'A cultural reawakening'

After my trip to Zutphen, I had an urge to visit my family in Sudan. Upon arriving at the airport, I immediately understood the pull that led me back. The sight of my parents at the arrivals terminal is a moment I will never forget.

Our reunion overflowed with pure love and gratitude. It felt as though decades had passed since we last saw each other, and all I wanted to do was shower them with affection and appreciation. The feeling of unconditional love was mutual. Despite our exhaustion from the late-night arrival, we stayed up talking and catching up until we all eventually fell asleep on my parents' giant bed.

My sensation of deep love and appreciation wasn't just felt towards my parents but everyone and everything I encountered. As I arrived at the house, an unfamiliar sensation of longing overcame me. I yearned for its familiar and soothing energy, the aroma of my mother's cooking, and the ever-present, bottomless coffee and tea awaited me. Every little thing ignited a spark of joy in my heart. I realised that with time, I had begun to forget how it made me feel.

Even things that once annoyed me, I began to perceive in a different light. When a neighbour or family member dropped by unannounced, I relished their genuine joy in seeing me. Being disconnected from it for years had made me see its beauty. No matter how long I stayed, saying goodbye to my parents had always been difficult. But that trip felt particularly challenging because I discerned a connection that I hadn't felt before.

It hit me, as I sat at the house's entrance watching passers-by, that it was essential to rebuild a connection to my roots to enhance my healing process, not only for my mind and body but for my heart and soul. Before departing from Khartoum, I carefully gathered small items that encapsulated the essence of my culture. These cherished possessions would accompany me wherever I travelled.

I would wake up each morning and engage in rituals that brought me closer to my heritage. The scent of Bakhoor filled the air, evoking a sense of nostalgia. I prepared Arabic coffee, savouring its rich flavour and the memories it stirred within me. As the aroma filled the room, I played a recitation from the Quran, just as we did back home. The sense of bliss and contentment that enveloped me through these simple acts was remarkable.

Alongside these items, I brought an array of local perfumes, jewellery, oils, and spices from Sudan, eager to indulge my senses and reconnect with the elements I had denied myself for far too long.

There was a belief that some of these items would be too foreign to incorporate into my current environment, but I was pleasantly surprised by the reception from my friends. As I adorned myself and my house with the unique fragrances, they would inquire with curiosity, 'What's that amazing smell?' Their appreciation for the distinctiveness of these scents warmed my heart. In fact, I often found myself sharing my Bakhoor with them, spreading the essence of my culture.

In addition to the olfactory delights, I rediscovered the joy of Sudanese and Middle Eastern music that had been absent for decades. The melodies and rhythms transported me back to my earlier days.

In 2017, early one morning, I crossed my legs and closed my eyes to meditate as part of my usual ritual. My brain was racing with thoughts, but it settled after a couple of breaths. As I sat in the stillness, an idea sparked in my mind. Why not host the very first Mindvalley event in the Middle East? While our focus had been on Western countries, where personal growth was becoming mainstream, the Middle East was largely untapped. But there was a catch. Back then, personal growth was not a topic taken seriously in the region. Many deemed it irrelevant; some even feared it would clash with their religious values. It was a risky move but one that could pay off immensely. Mindvalley had the potential to introduce personal growth to an entirely new audience and create a lasting impact.

I felt goosebumps on my skin at the idea. Without a second thought, I recorded a voice message to Mindvalley's founder: 'This might sound like a random idea, but we should do an event in the Middle East. Would love to talk to you more about why.'

I took a few minutes to stare at the recorded voice message before I finally clicked 'send.' My heart jumped with the click. I thought of everything that I had been immersed in for years, everything that had changed the course of my life—bringing it back to the region where I grew up instantly felt like a calling.

A few months later, I poured my heart and soul into a meticulously prepared pitch for the executive team. My efforts paid off when I received the coveted green light to lead our organization's inaugural event in the Middle East.

Two Worlds Mashed Up

Given the opportunity to lead the project, a newfound passion ignited within me. This endeavour was no mere work project; it felt like a personal mission I was destined to fulfill.

Simultaneously, I recognised the need to bridge the gap between these two distinct worlds I inhabited: the world I was raised in and the one I had built for myself. Until now, these aspects of my identity have remained separate. However, I realised it was time to integrate them fully, intertwining my personal and professional spheres.

Bringing Mindvalley to the Middle East felt akin to introducing a significant other to my family for the first time. It was like bringing someone from a completely different background who didn't speak the same language and was unfamiliar with the culture. The idea was undoubtedly daunting, but knowing that love was a shared value between both sides, I was determined to make the introduction.

After some research, I set my sights on the United Arab Emirates for the first event. I dived into the local business culture, connecting with different organizations and attending events to gain a deeper understanding of the region. Many concepts and ideas that Mindvalley put forward were considered advanced and relatively new. So, it was essential to determine the degree to which we presented these concepts.

In due course, the time arrived for us to be physically present, put our work to the test, and gauge the reception of Mindvalley by the locals. In 2018, we embarked on our first initiative, collaborating with an esteemed festival in Sharjah, a city that was transforming into an educational hub.

In 2019, we decided to be bolder and create a full Mindvalley experience in collaboration with the festival. A few months before the event, we were looking into creating an experience that would be relevant, meaningful, and appropriately aligned with the local culture and religious values. Knowing that the event would gather two thousand people, including the government, top organizations, and companies, it was vital to make an impact without getting lost in translation. I was meticulous with the agenda, briefing the speakers, and ensuring a seamless alignment.

My emotions were a whirlwind of thrill and apprehension. It wasn't just another task on my to-do list; it felt deeply personal. The stakes felt high, and the weight of responsibility was almost suffocating. I yearned for the two worlds I held dear to merge seamlessly, and the pressure to make it happen was immense. Perhaps my desperation stemmed from having poured every ounce of my being into pitching and fighting for this project. The fear of failure gnawed at me, despite my outward confidence. Doubts plagued my mind, questioning whether my vision was too ambitious and if my efforts would be in vain.

The event commenced, and we swung open the doors, inviting attendees to stream in. My heart buzzed as I witnessed the eager crowd rushing to secure seats closest to the stage. Their faces beamed with anticipation, filling me with a sense of exhilaration. In a matter of a few minutes, it was a full house.

The sound of Arabic dialects spoken by many individuals from the Middle East and North Africa washed over me, leaving me in awe. Here I was, pursuing my passion in the heart of the world I grew up in. It was an indescribable feeling. The host graciously welcomed the audience, and the energy in the room soared. I was introduced to give the opening speech. Standing before the attentive and loving crowd, I sensed a special connection forming. Their presence embraced me, allowing me to feel at ease and fully authentic in sharing my message.

What I didn't anticipate was the queue of remarkable men and women who came to tell me some of the most empowering words I had ever heard:

'Hi, Olla. I just came to tell you that your speech meant so much. Thank you for being so open and sharing with us....'

'You inspire me. To see a powerful Sudanese woman doing amazing things. You are a role model....'

'Thank you for bringing Mindvalley here. This is a dream come true.'

'I resonated with the message you shared. Thank you for that.'

The event was a success, opening a floodgate of new opportunities for us. We were invited to the most exclusive gatherings and meetings and received tremendous support everywhere we went. The synchronicities were abundant, and I was at the heart of it all. Although the pandemic caused setbacks, we were undaunted. We returned stronger, staging our biggest Mindvalley event yet in the UAE as soon as the world began to reopen. Thousands flocked to attend, and we were awed by the outpouring of support we received.

That experience transformed me in countless ways. It not only advanced my career but also imparted a vital life lesson. I used to think fitting in meant suppressing my individuality and conforming to the environment surrounding me. My background did not seem suited to my surroundings, so I suppressed it. But I realised this was a mistake.

Embracing my multiculturalism unlocked a new level of personal potential. It showed me that I don't have to compromise my identity to achieve success; instead, I found a deep sense of purpose and fulfillment by integrating my culture into every aspect of my life. My experience in Sharjah taught me the invaluable lesson that embracing who I am, has opened doors to opportunities and experiences that would have otherwise remained inaccessible. The more I appreciate my unique qualities, the more of my abilities I am able to tap into. It also inspired others to do the same. Above all, reconnecting with my roots rekindled a profound sense of connection to my soul. This renewed bond facilitated a heightened ability to attune to my soul's desires, making it easier to discern what truly resonated as meaningful and purposeful in my journey.

From
Tallinn

CHAPTER 11

FROM TALLINN

'A true home'

The pandemic hit like a tidal wave, sweeping away everything I knew as normal. Suddenly, my world was in chaos, and I felt like I was on a never-ending rollercoaster ride.

My job was no longer the same. My team was scattered, my role was redefined, the company culture was altered, and my travel calendar was empty. It was like starting from scratch, and it was a scary reality.

As the world came grinding to a halt, physical events became a thing of the past. Despite the global upheaval, I felt fortunate that Mindvalley chose to retain all its employees, even if it meant taking on different roles until the world reopened. Adapting to the new reality, however, was not without its challenges. It was an emotional rollercoaster to relinquish my previous role and be open to taking on any task that was needed. In retrospect, it taught me to detach from my job and be receptive to new experiences.

Amidst all the changes wrought by the pandemic, the most profound one was my unexpected relocation to Tallinn, Estonia.

As the lockdown in Malaysia tightened its grip, Vishen made a bold decision to relocate his family and some of the company's operations to Tallinn, Estonia, where another Mindvalley office was located. After careful consideration, a select few individuals who worked closely with him were chosen to join the team in Estonia. Ronan and I were among the chosen few.

Moving to a city that contrasted with our current home base immediately felt scary. However, upon examining the potential opportunities for a better quality of life and, most importantly, the possibility of finding a permanent place to call home, the benefits outweighed any apprehension we felt. Uncertainty loomed large, but a sense of adventure pulsed through me, urging me forward.

With my life compressed into a suitcase and a carry-on, I set out on an arduous journey to Tallinn with Ronan. Obtaining visas and navigating immigration had become a gruelling uphill battle as many embassies had closed their doors, and borders were heavily guarded. To secure an Estonian visa, I had to fly to Ankara to one of the few operating Estonian embassies. With only one appointment available that month, I had to pray fervently that I would make it to the appointment in time and receive my visa within the five-day window I had before my flight from Istanbul to Stockholm, where we had to clear immigration. The possibility of being denied entry at the European border was threatening, adding to the anxiety of an already risky journey.

Flights were scarce and unpredictable, and missing one would have disrupted the journey. Compounding the challenge was the fact that Malaysia's borders were closed, making it impossible to turn back. After years of traveling and feeling confident that I had overcome most challenges, this trip was a stark awakening. It felt like a mission impossible, taking the crown as one of the hardest ventures I had ever encountered. All the travel fears I thought I had conquered resurfaced and merged in this singular endeavour, intensifying its magnitude. It shattered my perception of facing the toughest trials and reminded me of the unpredictable nature of life's journey.

Our travel plans hit a snag when the first flight from Kuala Lumpur was cancelled 24 hours before departure. Frantic to find an alternative, I eventually managed to secure a flight that would get me to Ankara on time for my appointment.

Fortunately, I received my visa a day before my next flight to Stockholm. The eight-day journey to Tallinn was fraught with tension and uncertainty, and I found myself praying ceaselessly during the flight from Istanbul to Stockholm, hoping that we would be granted entry. With the grace of God, we eventually made it to Tallinn, safe and sound.

As soon as I stepped off the plane, a sense of relief washed over me that I had finally arrived at my destination. Traveling from one side of the world to another during the pandemic had been physically and emotionally draining. However, standing in the quaint and charming Tallinn airport felt incredibly rewarding. The warm welcome from my friends in the arrival hall made all the struggles instantly worth it. As we drove through the captivating streets of the old town, my friends took a risk by driving through areas where cars were prohibited, just to drop us off at our new home. As I stood in front of the 200-year-old building, I was awestruck by the stunning beauty of my new neighbourhood.

Compared to my experience in Malaysia, the pandemic restrictions in Tallinn were significantly less suffocating. Temperature checks were not required at every store, and masks were only mandatory indoors. Outdoor activities were encouraged, provided that social distancing was maintained. This allowed me to breathe fresh air without fear of breaking any laws. With nature adorning every corner of the city, I turned walking around Tallinn into my favourite form of entertainment. Every day, I explored my neighbourhood in awe, marvelling at the whimsical architecture, narrow cobblestone streets, ancient walls that once protected the city, and towering spires that rose from the skyline. It was as if I was living in my own movie! At times, I even forgot that there was a pandemic. Overall, moving to Tallinn was the best decision I could have made. Transitioning from a bustling metropolis to a tranquil city was the change I never knew I needed.

Out of the Familiar

When I announced my move to Estonia, reactions were a mixture of shock and disbelief. My European friends warned me about the infamous Estonian winters, but I was undeterred.

On my first day in Tallinn, I was met with the most beautiful surprise. Fluffy white snowflakes were falling from the sky, creating a winter wonderland before my eyes. I marvelled at the picturesque scenery and the peaceful serenity it brought to my soul. However, I soon realised that surviving the winter in Tallinn would take more than just admiring its beauty.

I had to learn the art of layering, finding the right shoes, and walking on snow without slipping. I felt like a little kid learning the basics of life all over again. And for some reason, I loved the presence and humility it brought.

I also had to train my mind to cope with the limited daylight hours and the darkness that seemed to cast a cloud over the city. But with the help of local friends and a deliberate effort to stay positive, I managed to navigate the coldest winters in Tallinn.

There were certainly challenges. Deciphering the weather, finding my way around the city, locating essential services like shops, gyms, hair salons, and cafes—this was all uncharted territory. And the biggest challenge? Everything was written in Estonian! Each product label in the supermarket was a puzzle, and I had to translate each word to know what I was about to consume.

In addition, with tourism being shut down during the pandemic, I found myself as the only minority on the streets, in stores, and even in restaurants. The locals were reserved and kept to themselves, making socializing and finding new friends difficult. But despite the obstacles, a strange comfort within me made me feel like I belonged. Although I didn't look like anyone, or understand the language, culture, or even the weather, I didn't feel like an outsider. It was as if Tallinn were calling out to me, inviting me to be a part of its community. Whenever someone asked me, 'How are you surviving the winter?' I would giggle and proudly say, 'I love it!' The surprise on their faces was priceless.

Over time, I slowly began to understand why a place like Tallinn, which would be unfamiliar and uncomfortable for many, offered me a sense of ease and belonging.

A True Home

For years, I had lived in countries where I felt like nothing more than a number. I had no rights, benefits, or laws that protected me. I constantly fought to fit in, and prove my worth. But everything changed when I moved to Estonia.

Two months after I arrived, I was granted a 5-year renewable residence permit. And with that residence came rights, benefits, and opportunities I had not experienced before. These included free healthcare, transport, and education, to name a few—privileges unheard of in any other country I had lived in, including the country where I was born.

For the first time in my life, I felt like I was genuinely contributing to society and that society was giving something back to me. I was no longer just an outsider living at the mercy of my visa.

After two happy years in Tallinn, my roots finally began to sink into the Earth, and my heart finally found its place. But I realised that there was much more to why this city made me feel I belonged, against all odds. It was all to do with how I felt inside. The years of battling to fit in and earn my place in the world led me to a deeper understanding of myself and a newfound love and acceptance of who I am. With the acceptance of myself, the world started to reflect the same.

I'd found a home in Tallinn because I'd found a home within myself.

Two years after I got my residency in Tallinn, I started my permanent residency in Brazil, but unexpectedly, received a ten-year residency in the United Arab Emirates. It no longer mattered what country I would live in, now or in the future. The hunt for an external home was over, as I'd rediscovered the one place that had always been my real home.

To bring my journey to a close, I still had one more place to go. The place where it all started.

From Home

EPILOGUE
FROM HOME

After eighteen years, it was time to return to the place where it all started. On an impulse, I booked a flight to Riyadh.

Upon arrival at the bustling King Khalid International Airport, I was greeted by my hometown's warm, familiar scent. I looked out the window at the yellow sandy field and felt a flood of emotions rising to the surface that was impossible to control. I finally let go of the tears queuing impatiently behind my eyelids.

My brother, Abbas, was waiting for me at the arrival hall. The sight of him filled me with unbridled joy. It had been three years since I saw him last, but Abbas never changed. He wore his favourite colour, black, from head to toe, with matching sunglasses. You would mistake him for Will Smith in *Men in Black* from a distance. His height, skin colour, and the features of his face were similar, but Abbas has kind brown eyes and soft brown hair.

As we made our way to the city, we caught up on old times, reminiscing about our childhood in Riyadh and how it had shaped our lives. The city came into view, and I was mesmerized. I could see Al Faisaliah Tower from a distance, once the tallest building in Riyadh, now standing amidst a sea of skyscrapers in a city that had changed drastically. The sight of women driving was just one of the many changes that made it difficult to connect the city of my memories to the one right in front of me.

With a sudden urge, I turned to Abbas and asked, 'Can we pass by Al Salhiya?'

'Al Salhiya? Right now?' Abbas replied, confused.

'Yes, please. Just for a few minutes,' I responded, hopeful.

'What do you want to do there?'

'Honestly, I don't know, but I feel this urge to go there now.'

Abbas shrugged and replied cheerfully, 'Sure thing.' He drove to Al Salhiya, the building that housed our five-bedroom apartment. He parked and waited for me in his car. I walked inside the building, continued to the elevator, and pressed the number six. I stepped out on the sixth floor and approached what used to be my family's apartment.

I felt as if my muscles were beginning to give up one after the other. I kneeled as I approached the doorstep. It was as though I was meeting a forgotten part of me after eighteen years of separation. Sitting beside the apartment I had once called home, I was overcome by a tsunami of memories—childhood, family, friends, and everything in between.

Suddenly, my mind went silent, and my heart followed. No more thoughts, no feelings. I was just ... present.

As I sat in silence, my life journey came into focus.

Growing up with immigrant parents in a multicultural environment, I struggled with my identity, constantly switching between different facets to fit in. For decades, I searched for a sense of belonging, forcing myself into boxes and never finding balance or wholeness.

But then, in a moment of clarity, I realised that my identity is a unique and beautiful blend of my heritage and experiences. All my travels, from Riyadh to Rio, had a deeper purpose—to find that truth. In each place, I encountered new challenges and discoveries that helped me come closer to myself.

In Khartoum, I learned to trust my instincts to pursue an unconventional path that changed the course of my life.

In Kuala Lumpur, I embraced the unknown and discovered a world of possibilities beyond my imagination.

In Puerto Vallarta, I learned that my self-worth was not defined by how others perceived me.

In Dubrovnik, I began a healing journey to let go of the past and embrace the present.

In Miami, I learned to embrace acceptance amidst rejection and discovered the potency of compassion toward myself and those around me.

In Rio, I understood that prioritizing love is vital when making tough decisions.

In San Diego, I discovered the power of speaking my truth and shifting my weakness into power.

In Zutphen, I started loving relationships with my mind and body.

In Sharjah, I had a cultural reawakening, reunited with my roots, and built a stronger connection to my identity.

In Tallinn, I experienced a sense of inner peace and belonging.

Every city I visited redirected me back to self-love and helped me find a sense of home within myself. But it was when I sat on the floor of the apartment of my hometown, that a revelation as bright as daylight emerged:

Having journeyed through more than 90 countries, all those years of exploration to find a place to call home had little to do with the countries, their climates, cuisines, or people. I couldn't feel at home for all those years because I wasn't home in my body, mind, heart, and soul. Lacking acceptance in one or multiple areas of these crucial aspects of my existance, eluded me from feeling at home no matter where I went.

For years, I subjected my body to bullying and neglect, failing to appreciate the very vessel that had been my constant companion. Despite spending my entire life housed within it, the lack of acceptance didn't make me feel at home within my body. Only when I nurtured a renewed bond, fostering acceptance and genuine appreciation, did I finally find that sense of belonging within my own skin. I started to find a home within my body.

In moments consumed by relentless, negative thoughts—those whispers that repeated 'you are not enough'—my mind wasn't a sanctuary of belonging. Regardless of my location or experiences, my mind held the power to convince me that I didn't fit in, reinforcing the notion that I didn't belong. My journey led me to delve deep into my mind to work on reshaping my thoughts and thereby discovering a true sense of home within my mind.

The chambers of my heart long remained an unexplored territory, tainted by resentment, anger, blame, and a shortage of self-love. To cultivate a sense of home, I realised the need to unearth, relinquish, and continuously forgive, creating space for love to flow in freely. With self-love, I began to find a home within my heart.

During those phases of disconnection and uncertainty – times when purpose seemed distant, and my faith wavered – my soul yearned for a place to call home. Working on rekindling my roots, understanding my identity, and strengthening my spiritual bond breathed life back into my soul's dwelling. Through this journey of self-discovery, I unlocked the gates to a true home, a residence for the soul where I could find solace and purpose.

At last, I grasped the life-changing truth that the concept of home far surpasses mere physical coordinates. Home is the process of returning to acceptance within my body, mind, heart, and soul. It stands not as a fixed destination but rather as an ongoing journey, an ever-evolving pilgrimage throughout the entirety of my life.

It is the process of cultivating a sense of home within myself, on those days when I wake up uncertain of my purpose, when I achieve my goals but still feel a sense of emptiness, when faced with condescending remarks, or when I struggle to feel gratitude amidst abundance. It is in these moments that I find solace and strength, knowing that it is all part of the process and the answers will always come from the home within.

The journey from Riyadh to Rio, through different cultures, relationships, religions, and love, has taught me that I haven't arrived at my destination; I am just about to begin finding the next one.

ACKNOWLEDGEMENTS

I am deeply grateful for the moment I held this book in my hands. However, I wouldn't be here without the unwavering support and belief of those who cheered me on at every stage. First and foremost, I want to express my heartfelt appreciation to my husband, Ronan, who consistently referred to me as 'his favourite author' even before I had a book in hand. Your constant love and relentless faith in this work have been my pillars. Thank you.

I owe a debt of gratitude to Rajesh Setty, who planted the seed of the idea to write a book and encouraged me to see it through. Thank you for recognising something in my story before I could see it myself.

To my parents, the source of boundless and unparalleled love, you are my world. To my sister, Alyaa, you are the very breath in my lungs. Hamodi, thank you for bringing endless joy to my heart. To my siblings, Assgad, Abbas, and Attaf, I am truly blessed to have you in my life. And to my cousins Shahad, Wijdan, Yaqeen, Maab, and Tajweed, your unconditional love has meant everything to me. May, Sandra, Jose, thank you for taking me in with so much love. To Mina, Firas, and Basbos, my love for all of you is immeasurable.

To my global family: Lux Anne, your presence in my life is a precious gift. Your kindness and grace inspire me every day. Fuad, thank you for standing by my side through thick and thin. Vadim, Guatum, Alessio and Alsu, I am so grateful to have you. Razan and Rudy, you always make my heart smile. Loubna and Ibtehal, I am blessed to have our paths crossed. Thabit and Amir, my Sudanese gang, I cherish the fact that we began an amazing journey together. You all will always be family.

To my Mindvalley family: Vishen, you have played an instrumental role in some of the most transformative experiences of my life. Your kindness, love, and unwavering support over the years are difficult to put into words. I deeply appreciate you. Kadi, my sister from another mister, your presence brings joy to my soul. Thank you for simply being you. MamaLaura, your kindness knows no bounds. Thank you for your love and care. Alvaro, Tiina, Miriam, and Kaia, I appreciate you. Kristina and Masha, thank you for your loving support. Tanya, you are a constant source of inspiration, and I consider myself truly blessed to have you. Jason Campbell, Sammy T, and Jason G, your encouragement had always made me feel loved. Hannah, you were among the first to believe in me, and I have always admired your fierce determination.

To the team that contributed to this book: Mustafa, thank you for your kindness towards me and the rest of the team. Amy and Gigi, thank you for being among the first to support. Karen, your stunning photograph, captured without my knowledge, has become the perfect cover. Chee, thank you for always stepping in to rescue my less-than-stellar designs.

FROM HOME

A shout out for the photos from unsplash used for chapter covers by Safaa Almohandis, Thana Gu, Miguel Naranjo, Adam Thomas, Derek Story, Rosan Harmens, Saj Shafique, Jaanus Jagomägi, Clay Banks. As well as Samcoldest and Rachel Claire images on Pexels.

Lastly, I extend my gratitude to everyone I have crossed paths with, who offered an encouraging word, shared an idea, or taught me a valuable lesson that contributed to the creation of this volume. And to you for demonstrating love simply by being here.

Thank you all.

Connect with Me

@olla.abbas on Instagram

Notes

....

....

....

....

....

....

....

....

....

....

....

....

....

....

....

Milton Keynes UK
Ingram Content Group UK Ltd.
UKHW040959040324
438885UK00005B/327